LUTHERANISM

[*Lutheranismus*]

That is,

Luther's Catechism

Briefly explained through question and answer
And set against the most prominent Calvinistic objections.

First printed in Hamburg,
Now reviewed and in many ways
Increased and improved
In this Evangelical Jubilee Year.

by

Jacob Martini,

Professor at the Honorable University of Wittenberg.

Printed by Johan Nahtzow, Published by Paul Zelswig's
bookshop there.
Anno 1618.

Repristination Press
Malone, Texas

First edition, December 2024.

REPRISTINATION PRESS
716 HCR 3424 E
MALONE, TEXAS 76660

www.repristinationpress.com

ISBN (10) 1-891469-87-8
ISBN (13) 9781891469879

Table of Contents

Foreword to the English Translation.

It is a joy to publish a volume from the works of Jacob Martini (1570–1649). Although nowhere near as well known as the more prominent theologians of his period, Martini was a prominent Lutheran theologian and philosopher during the late 16th and early 17th centuries. Born in Halberstadt, Germany, Martini played a significant role in the development of Lutheran Orthodoxy during a period marked by theological and philosophical challenges to the Reformation's legacy. He studied at the University of Wittenberg, the epicenter of Lutheran thought, where he would later teach and become one of its key figures. In 1593, Jakob Martini acquired a Master's degree at the University of Wittenberg. Under Polykarp Leyser the Elder and Aegidius Hunnius he grew in his knowledge of theology, and in 1597 he took a teaching position in Norden, which also came with a pastoral appointment. He returned to Wittenberg in 1602 and served in a series of professorships for the remainder of his life, attaining his doctorate in 1623.

Martini is perhaps best known for his contributions to defending Lutheran doctrines against both Roman Catholic and Reformed (Calvinist) critiques. His theological writings reflect his commitment to the *Book of Concord* (1580), which is foundational for Lutheran orthodoxy. He emphasized the authority of Scripture and the central tenets of justification by faith alone, maintaining a strict adherence to the Lutheran confessional standards.

In addition to his theological work, Martini was deeply engaged with the philosophical discourse of his time. His use of logical rigor and academic disputations made him a respected voice in theological debates. His notable abilities in this regard are readily in evidence at various points in *Lutheranismus*. Modern readers will no doubt find portions of this work to be quite challenging. Consideration was given to providing an extensive commentary on his use of philosophical technical language. However, it was feared that such extensive commentary would detract, or at least distract, from the text.

Martini's role as an academician was significant. As a professor at Wittenberg, he trained future Lutheran pastors, ensuring the transmission of orthodox Lutheran doctrine to subsequent generations. His influence extended through both his teaching and his published works, which served as tools for theological education and polemics.

Jacob Martini's legacy lies in his steadfast defense of Lutheran orthodoxy and his contributions to the intellectual tradition of the Lutheran Reformation, particularly during a time when it faced significant external and internal pressures. He remains an important figure in the history of Lutheran theology and philosophy.

One other representative sample of Martini's work has thus far been translated into English, *A Contentious Question (Streitige Frage): Whether the Godhead is truly known to some degree, or may indeed be known by human understanding without the revealed Word? (1619)* which was published by the Center for the Study of Lutheran Orthodoxy in 2012.

At present, it seems unlikely that there will be substantial increase in the number of Martini's works being made available in English. However, it is hoped that this slender volume will awaken the interest and imagination of Lutherans of the current generation.

Rt. Rev. James D. Heiser, M.Div., S.T.M.
Bishop, the ELDoNA
Pastor, Salem Lutheran Church (Malone, Texas)
Festival of St. Thomas, Apostle, A.D. 2024

To the Most Serene and Illustrious Princess and Lady, Lady Hedwig, Born of the Royal Line of Denmark, Duchess of Saxony, Jülich, Cleves, and Berg, Electress, Landgravine of Thuringia, Margravine of Meissen, Countess of the Mark and Ravensburg, Lady of Ravenstein, Widow,

My Most Gracious Electress and Lady.*

Grace and peace to you in this New Year from God the Father and the Lord Jesus Christ.

Most Serene and Illustrious Electress, Most Gracious Lady,

The Holy Apostle Peter, in his First Epistle, chapter three, admonishes and commands all Christians, saying: "Always be ready to give an answer to everyone who asks you to give the reason for the hope that you have, and do so with gentleness and respect," etc. In these words, the Holy Apostle requires two things of us:

Firstly, that we rightly know and understand the articles of the Christian faith, their foundation, and their proofs.

Secondly, that we should be ready and courageous, when necessity demands, to give an account and answer to anyone concerning these articles of our faith, in which our true and

* Hedwig of Denmark (1581–1641) was the daughter of King Frederick II of Denmark and Sophie of Mecklenburg-Güstrow. As the wife of Christian II (1583–1611), Hedwig was Electress of Saxony from 1602 to 1611. The marriage was childless, and her husband was succeeded by his brother John George. However, even after the death of Christian II, Hedwig retained a great deal of power and influence in Saxony.

certain hope is grounded. This division is both beautifully and well-made, as these two aspects encompass all that pertains to our Christianity.

The first encompasses the Christian faith, which alone justifies and makes a person a true Christian. Although the formal and essential nature, essence, and being of this faith consist in placing true trust in the merit of our Lord Jesus Christ and applying and appropriating it to oneself, nevertheless, this trust must have a firm foundation and ground. This foundation is *notitia,* the *knowledge* of what God the Lord has revealed to us in His holy Word concerning His essence and will. Following this is *assensus,* namely, that we *firmly hold* and are assured that what has been revealed and prescribed to us in the Word is the holy, immutable, and imperishable divine truth.

For if I am to firmly grasp the heavenly goods that Christ Jesus has obtained for me, I must know wherein they consist, how they are to be grasped and obtained, and furthermore, since I cannot study and attain them through nature and reason but must learn of them solely from divine revelations set forth in His Word, I must also be certain and doubt not in the least that the revelations and promises in the Word are indeed God's revelations and promises. From this follows the inner *trust* and *fiducia* in our Lord and Savior Jesus Christ, and through Him, in God, His heavenly Father, together with the Holy Spirit, who works such trust in our hearts through the Word, increases, establishes, confirms, sanctifies, and preserves it. And this is why we commonly describe true Christian faith as follows: *Fides est notitia, assensus, et fiducia*—"Faith is knowledge, assent, and inner trust." For if we are to always trust in God, we must assent to His Word, wherein He has revealed Himself and made His essence and will known. If we are to assent to this Word, we must know what is written in it and what the articles of faith to which we are to assent and hold as true encompass. This is what the Apostle Paul says in Romans 10: "*Fides ex auditu est*"—Faith comes from hearing, and hearing through the Word of God. Thus, the Apostle wills that, in due order, faith arises from hearing the Word of God. For through hearing, our understanding is opened, and we are made to recognize and know what we could never attain through our own efforts or powers.

Because the preached and heard Word of God is a *vehiculum* and channel of the Holy Spirit, He thereby enters into our hearts and minds, ignites in them a new light and a new knowledge, guiding us into all truth and revealing what He has heard from the Father and the Son. But He does not stop there; He accomplishes much more, for He warms our cold and unbelieving stony hearts, makes them believing, and entirely softens them so that what we have learned and know, we recognize from the depths of our hearts, firmly and steadfastly assent to it, and, in genuine, fervent trust, through Christ Jesus, turn to the true God, approach His gracious and fatherly presence, and, in firm hope, call upon Him, saying: "Abba, dear Father."

This true faith cannot exist alone; rather, it is immediately followed, *ut effectus immediatus suam causam* ("as an immediate effect follows its cause"), by the new obedience. For just as the sun does not exist without its glorious, beautiful, and bright rays that illuminate heaven and earth, so, too, true Christian faith cannot exist without the new obedience. This new obedience consists of all kinds of glorious, beautiful, spiritual virtues that, like radiant and beautiful sunbeams, emanate from it and illuminate the entire holy Christian Church—indeed, making it shine brightly and splendidly throughout the whole world.

The foremost virtue among all is *Fortitudo Christiana*, Christian courage or bravery. For, as is commonly said of fortitude in ethical writings, that it not only encompasses justice but also all other virtues, supports them, and serves as their bulwark and reinforcement, so too can it be rightly said of Christian fortitude. It includes the justice of faith, true love for God, proper and true worship of God, and all other Christian virtues. It confesses these openly, without fear, from the depths of the heart and with steadfast courage, defends them, and indeed, if necessary, testifies and confirms them with body, blood, and death. Thus, it is willingly and unhesitatingly ready, as required, to give an account of the true faith and does not fear friend or foe, love or hate, honor or dishonor, life or death. For it knows that the Apostle's word in Romans 10 is true: "If one believes with the heart, one is justified; and if one confesses with the mouth, one is saved." Although this confession does not merit or earn eternal salvation—because we are justified and saved solely through faith in Christ—this, too, aligns with the Apostle's declaration in Ephesians 2:8: "By grace, you have been saved through faith, and this is not of yourselves; it is the gift of God, not of works, so that no one may boast." Yet, where this confession and profession of faith is found, there also is true faith. For this confession and *Fortitudo Christiana* (Christian courage) are the undeniable effects of true faith and remain, as its inseparable companions, always joined to it. This is why the Lord Christ Himself says in Matthew 10:33: "Whoever confesses Me before men, I will also confess before My Father in heaven; but whoever denies Me before men, I will also deny before My Father in heaven." Similarly, the Apostle says in 2 Timothy 2:13: "If we deny Him, He will also deny us." Therefore, if we are to be true Christians, we must be ready to confess the Lord Christ before the world, even at the risk of life and limb. We must never allow ourselves to be moved away from Him or to fear those who can kill the body but cannot kill the soul. Rather, we must fear Him who can destroy both body and soul in hell. We should know that the reward in heaven will be great for those who endure persecution for the sake of righteousness (Matthew 5). For those who overcome will be given to eat from the tree of life, which is in the paradise of God, and from the hidden manna. They will be given a good testimony and the testimony of a new name written, which no one knows except the one who receives it. They will be clothed in white garments, and their name will not be erased from the Book of Life (Revelation 1 and 2). As we read of the exceedingly great and innumerable multitude of holy martyrs in Revelation 7, we see their example, their faith, and their steadfast confession that serve as a beacon for the entire Christian Church.

Likewise, the royal prophet David, driven by this heroic and truly Christian virtue, declares in Psalm 116: "I believe, therefore I speak." This teaches us that it is not enough to carry true faith hidden in the heart; it must also lead to public and genuine confession or profession of faith. Thus, the ancient Church Father, Augustine, rightly and aptly states that those who do not publicly confess their faith do not have true faith, for true faith necessarily includes the conviction to believe the Lord Christ, who says: "Whoever confesses Me before men, I will also confess before My Father in heaven."

Just as David, in the aforementioned Psalm, laments that he is greatly afflicted, so, too, must true believers, in their confession and on account of it, expect persecutions and all kinds of crosses and adversities—even death itself—just as the Lord Christ has previously told them in Matthew 10: "You will be hated for My name's sake." And yet, even so, just as David, in the midst of mortal danger, speaks with joyful, steadfast, and courageous spirit: "*Credidi, propter quod locutus sum*"—"I believed; therefore, I spoke"—so must we also, in no cross or adversity, despair or even grieve in the slightest. Instead, we must be strong and courageous, speak the truth boldly, and confess it openly and without hesitation, because we truly believe.

It is therefore certain that whoever possesses true faith does not shy away from making their confession, publicly professing their faith, and defending it.

The question then arises: to whom are we obligated to make our confession and give an account of our faith? The Apostle teaches us this immediately in the following words when he says: "To everyone who asks you for the reason for the hope that is in you." Just as every virtue consists in *mediocritas* (moderation), so the Apostle wishes to teach us further that this also applies to *Fortitudo Christiana* (Christian fortitude), from which flows an unhesitating confession and profession of faith. Therefore, in order to maintain this moderation, two extremes must be avoided:

- The first, which resides in defect, is *timiditas* (fear),
- The second, which errs in excess, is *audacia, temeritas* (boldness, rashness), or what can be called impudence, recklessness, or presumption.

Then there are the *audaculi*, the rash and exceedingly presumptuous, who, without being asked or prompted, at all times and in all places, without distinction, whether under the influence of beer and wine, acting wildly and irrationally, or sober and in sound mind, in inappropriate settings, boast of all they know or think they know. Whether out of pride, arrogance, and presumption—as if they alone knew everything about religion—they chatter, debate, judge, vex, and agitate others, seeking to reform everyone. Alternatively, out of ignorance, recklessness, and bad habits, they fail to honor God or act for the good of their conscience or for the edification of their neighbor. Instead, out of sheer frivolity, they mock God or confuse and trouble their neighbor, turning matters of religion into meaningless or vain talk, jesting, or foolishness.

This is not the intent of the Holy Apostle. He does not

call for indiscriminate talk but instead commands us to answer only those who ask for the reason for the hope that is in us. For this reason, God has endowed His own with the *spiritu discretionis* (spirit of discernment) so that they may know and judge rightly when, how, to what extent, to whom, and in which settings it is necessary to speak of divine matters. Indeed, as is otherwise well-established, Christ Himself says and commands in Matthew 7:6: "Do not give what is holy to dogs, and do not throw your pearls before swine, lest they trample them underfoot and turn to attack you." Likewise, the Apostle Paul, in 1 Timothy 6:20, admonishes us to avoid *ungodly chatter* and quarrels with those who lack faith.

Therefore, the entire sum of this apostolic command is that we must always have our confession or profession of faith ready so that we can present it publicly when necessity requires it; namely, when there is a hope to be declared, when the honor of God demands it, or when, for certain reasons, one must confess the name of the Lord Christ. For at such times, it is not the moment to remain silent or to conceal our faith.

Just as *Fortitudo Christiana* (Christian fortitude) is the foremost virtue, as stated above, so too must its effect, which is *confessio* (confession), be entirely free of vice and adorned with all manner of Christian virtues. Above all, according to the teaching of the Holy Apostle, these two virtues should shine forth and be most evident: *gentleness* and *fear of God*.

Gentleness excludes anger, excessive clamor, outrageous slander, and unchristian insults, which serve only to create unwarranted offenses in the Christian Church and make adversaries all the more stubborn and unyielding.

Closely joined with gentleness is *Reverentia erga Deum*, or *Timor Dei*—the *fear of God*. Where this fear is present, it utterly condemns all arrogance of the heart and enables us to rightly and gently handle the mysteries of God. For it teaches us that if we are to properly present the confession of our faith to the Lord God, there must be no pride or vainglory, nor any hatred, envy, or discord found among us.

Thus, certain foolishness is rightly rejected and entirely condemned, especially when individuals cannot speak or discuss matters concerning the Lord Christ, the holy religion, or what pertains to it, except, as mentioned, in public taverns over beer or wine. When their noses are soaked with wine or beer, their minds no longer know what to think, nor their tongues what to say. Or, they speak of Christ and debate in such a way that it ultimately leads *à verbis ad verbera*—from verbal disputes to fistfights. In such cases, it is supposedly well-accomplished: the name of God has been "greatly honored," and the confession has been "mightily proclaimed." But believe me, dear Christian, such a confession is not pleasing to God, for it is not done with gentleness and true fear of God, which the Apostle requires here. Nevertheless, this does not mean we are speaking against legitimate reproofs and corrections of the godless and their false teachings. For the zeal of the prophets and the earnestness of the apostles in correcting and admonishing are well known.

Finally, it is important to note in this precept of the Apostle Peter that his intention is not that we should be ready to answer every question, regardless of its nature. Not at all—far from it. For it is not everyone's duty to immediately have an answer to every question, or to discuss and deliberate on every argument and matter. Rather, the Apostle is speaking here about the general teaching, which is accessible even to the unlearned and simple-minded. Specifically, we are to give an answer to those who ask for the reason for the hope that is in us. The Apostle intends nothing other than that we Christians should demonstrate and prove to the unbelievers that we honor God rightly with pure hearts and hold our religion as sacred. There is no great difficulty in this, for it would indeed be most unreasonable if we were entirely unable to answer someone who inquires about our faith.

Indeed, in consideration and reflection of this, the Reverend Luther, early in the Reformation of our churches, composed his *Small Catechism*, succinctly summarizing the foundations of our Christian faith, worship, and doctrine, and presenting it to the common man in the form of a table. This was intended to make it easy for him to grasp and, as circumstances and necessity arose, to provide a simple yet accurate confession of his faith. Through this, the Reverend Luther accomplished great benefit and dealt a powerful blow to the papacy. For previously, under the papacy, the common man knew almost nothing about his faith or Christianity. Instead, he was led to believe that it was sufficient to possess an *implicitam fidem* (implicit faith), with his belief wrapped up in the common Catholic faith—this being contrary to the Word of God, which declares: "The righteous shall live by faith."

As I say, under the papacy, the common man—this included princes, lords, kings, and all worldly rulers—was led by the nose and shamefully deceived. Consequently, according to the Apostle's teaching, he was unable to give any answer to someone who inquired of him or asked for the reason for the hope that should have been certain within him. Instead, he could only say that he believed whatever the Roman Church believed. Through this booklet, however, the eyes of everyone were opened. They no longer trusted or believed in the abomination of Babylon but were instead able to give a clear and correct answer to anyone who asked for the foundation of their hope and faith.

It happened some years ago, when I was in service with the Counts of East Frisia, that, along with three other Lutheran preachers and pastors, we were tasked, for certain reasons, to produce a written confession in the name of the Lutheran churches of East Frisia. This was to be done according to the structure of the Augsburg Confession, specifying the articles in which we agree with the so-called Zwinglians or Calvinists and those in which we still have disagreements. This task was imposed and commanded by the high authorities of the region. Recalling the words and directive of the holy Apostle Peter, we did not deliberate long but promptly and correctly explained all the articles of the Augsburg Confession. Since I was the unworthy one wielding the pen at that time, the draft of that document remains in my possession to this day.

However, because our confession was not written to suit everyone's wishes or preferences (since some were hoping for a new Interim*), our work was set aside. Nevertheless, this matter became known throughout the Lutheran churches in East Frisia, and among many prominent and high-ranking individuals within the region. As a result, some claimed one thing and others another regarding our confession, misinterpreting it, and even those who were of our persuasion were somewhat unsettled and confused. Consequently, I was urged to compose a short instruction on the Calvinian controversy, following the framework of our catechism, so that it would not appear as though we intended to forcibly publish the written confession. Instead, the goal was to provide some guidance to the common people. Recalling the command of Peter once more, I willingly undertook this task, compiled this booklet briefly, published it,

* Martini references the infamous Augsburg Interim (1548–1552), through which Emperor Charles V sought to undo the Lutheran Reformation through oppression of faithful teachers, suppression of Lutheran practices, and corruption of adiaphoristic practices to ease a transition back to Papal control of the Lutheran churches. The effort was brought to a end by the successful uprising of Maurice of Saxony and the Peace (1552) and Treaty of Augsburg (1555).

and had it printed in Hamburg for the benefit of the common people.

However, since the copies had long been dispersed but were nevertheless desired by many devout people, I, at the urging of several of my good friends, took this booklet back into my hands during this Evangelical Jubilee Year.* I carefully reviewed, corrected, slightly expanded, and improved it—primarily for the purpose of once again publicly declaring my faith and demonstrating to all Christendom that my theological and philosophical labors, which, without boasting, I have pursued with the utmost diligence and not without harm to my health, as is widely known, have been carried out over the past sixteen years at this esteemed University of Wittenberg, both publicly and privately**. As much as God grants me grace and as my health permits, I shall continue to pursue these efforts, directed and devoted entirely to honoring God, advancing the true religion and Christianity, and building up the beloved youth.

I now hear also of Your Electoral Grace, who is descended from the royal lineage of the northern peoples, that in you, as well, this glorious prophecy of the Reverend Luther has been fulfilled in a Christian and praiseworthy manner. You hold the Christian religion in the highest regard, daily engage in the study of God's Word, and have so firmly laid the foundation of divine truth that you are thoroughly and rightly able to distinguish truth from falsehood, right from wrong. Thus, you are able, in accordance with the Apostle's command, to give an account and provide a well-grounded answer and instruction to anyone—whether learned or unlearned—who inquires of the foundation of your faith. You can also powerfully defend

---

* A.D. 1617 was observed as the centennial of the Lutheran Reformation.

** Martini was called to Wittenberg in 1602 to teach Philosophy and Metaphysics. In 1613 he became the professor of Ethics, and formally joined the theological faculty after being awarded his doctorate in 1623.

the true religion from God's Word. Such dedication is highly commendable in royal, electoral, and princely persons and noblewomen, and therefore should be praised by all, and held up as exemplary for Christendom, that many may see it as a shining example.

Just as I, for this reason, wished to dedicate the first edition of this booklet to the esteemed princess in God, now deceased, from East Frisia, who at that time was my gracious princess and lady, so now, for the very same reason, I wish to dedicate this revised and entirely new edition to Your Electoral Grace, my most gracious electress and lady, in the most humble reverence, and present it as a gift for a blessed New Year. I am in the humblest hope that Your Electoral Grace will graciously regard this work. Finally, from the depths of my heart, I wish Your Electoral Grace a joyful and blessed New Year, enduring health, long life, and every other temporal and eternal blessing from Almighty God.

Given in Wittenberg on New Year's Day of the year 1618.

Your Electoral Grace's
most humble servant,
Jacobus Martini.

The First Part
Concerning the Law of God.

Matthew 22.

"You shall love the Lord your God with all your heart, with all your soul, and with all your mind. This is the first and greatest commandment. And the second is like it: You shall love your neighbor as yourself. On these two commandments hang all the Law and the Prophets."

1. *How many parts are there in our Christian Catechism?*

Six.

The first deals with the Law of God, or the Holy Ten Commandments.

The second, with the Articles of the Christian Faith.

The third, with Prayer, as Christ has taught and commanded us to pray.

The fourth, with the Sacrament of Holy Baptism.

The fifth, with the Office of the Keys, Confession, and Absolution.

The sixth, with the Sacrament of the True Body and Blood of our Lord Jesus Christ.

Concerning the Law of God. Or Holy Ten Commandments.

2. *From the title, I understand that these are ten commandments. Into how many tables are they divided?*

Into two.

3. *What does the First Table concern?*

The love of God. For the Lord Christ summarized it briefly in Matthew 22: "You shall love the Lord your God with all your heart, with all your soul, and with all your mind."

4. *What does the Second Table concern?*

The love of one's neighbor. For the Lord Christ summarized it briefly once again, saying: "You shall love your neighbor as yourself." And He further adds: "On these two commandments hang all the Law and the Prophets."

5. *How many commandments are in the First Tablet?*

Three.

The First Commandment

"You shall have no other gods before Me."

What does this mean?

Answer: We should fear, love, and trust in God above all things.

The Second Commandment

"You shall not misuse the name of the Lord your God."

What does this mean?

Answer: We should fear and love God so that we do not curse, swear, practice witchcraft, lie, or deceive by His name, but call upon it in every trouble, pray, praise, and give thanks.

The Third Commandment

"Remember the Sabbath day by keeping it holy."

What does this mean?

Answer: We should fear and love God so that we do not despise preaching and His Word, but regard it as holy and gladly hear and learn it.

6. *How many commandments are in the second table?*

Seven.

The Fourth Commandment

"Honor your father and your mother, that it may go well with you and you may live long on the earth."

What does this mean?

Answer: We should fear and love God so that we do not despise or anger our parents and rulers, but honor them, serve them, obey them, and hold them in love and esteem.

The Fifth Commandment

"You shall not kill."

What does this mean?

Answer: We should fear and love God so that we do not harm or hurt our neighbor in his body, but help and support him in every bodily need.

The Sixth Commandment

"You shall not commit adultery."

What does this mean?

Answer: We should fear and love God so that we lead a chaste and decent life in words and deeds, and each loves and honors his spouse.

The Seventh Commandment

"You shall not steal."

What does this mean?

Answer: We should fear and love God so that we do not take our neighbor's money or possessions, or acquire them by dishonest dealing, but help him to improve and protect his possessions and income.

The Eighth Commandment

"You shall not bear false witness against your neighbor."

What does this mean?

Answer: We should fear and love God so that we do not deceitfully lie about, betray, slander, or give a bad reputation to our neighbor, but instead we should excuse him, speak well of him, and interpret everything in the best possible way.

The Ninth Commandment

"You shall not covet your neighbor's house."

What does this mean?

Answer: We should fear and love God so that we do not scheme to get our neighbor's inheritance or house, or obtain it in a way that appears right, but instead be of help and service to him in keeping it.

The Tenth Commandment

"You shall not covet your neighbor's wife, servant, maid, livestock, or anything that is his."

What does this mean?

Answer: We should fear and love God so that we do not entice or force away our neighbor's wife, servants, or livestock, but urge them to stay and do their duty.

7. What does God say about all these commandments?

Answer: He says thus: "I, the LORD your God, am a strong, jealous God, who visits the sins of the fathers upon the children to the third and fourth generation of those who hate me, but shows mercy and goodness to thousands of generations of those who love me and keep my commandments."

What does this mean?

Answer: God threatens to punish all who transgress these commandments; therefore, we should fear His wrath and not act against such commandments. However, He promises grace and all good things to those who keep such commandments; therefore, we should also love Him, trust Him, and willingly act according to His commandments.

8. Why, then, do you not, like the Calvinists, count four commandments in the first table? Such that the first would be: "You shall have no other gods"; the second, "You shall make no graven image"; the third, "You shall not misuse the name of God"; and the fourth, "You shall keep the Sabbath holy"; and why do you not combine the ninth and tenth into one commandment in the second table?

Counting the Ten Commandments in this way or another is a misunderstanding that neither adds to, nor takes away from, the Ten Commandments. Therefore, it is an unnecessary dispute stirred up by the Calvinists.

9. How do you prove that the division of the Ten Commandments belongs to things of indifference?

I prove this with three reasons:

First, Moses, in Exodus 20 and Deuteronomy 5, did not specify the number, which he would undoubtedly have done if it had been of great importance, for the Holy Spirit has left nothing out that entails divine necessity.

Second, the holy apostles themselves exercised this freedom and took the liberty to arrange the commandments differently. , In Romans 13, the Apostle Paul places the sixth commandment before the fifth, which he would not have done if the numbering and order were so essential.

Third, the Lord Christ Himself did not observe the numbering strictly. When He recounted the Ten Commandments to the young man who asked what he must keep to be saved by the Law, He mentioned the commandment regarding obedience to parents last. The Lord would not have done this if there were such a great necessity in the numbering.

10. Even if I accept all of this as valid, Luther should not have followed his own judgment or the traditions and decrees of the Papists. Rather, he should have observed how the early Church Fathers divided the Ten Commandments. For Origen, Gregory of Nazianzus, Ambrose, Jerome, and others divided the Ten Commandments as the current Calvinists do.

As for the holy Fathers and church teachers, their authority is rightly held in honor, and we do not fault them for dividing the Ten Commandments in such a way, placing four commandments in the first tablet. However, they did not compel anyone to adhere to such a division and numbering, as the Calvinists seek to do now. It is also worth noting that the distinction and division made by Luther was not spun from his own mind, much less taken from Papal decrees. Instead, it is a very viable arrangement, already in use by the later Augustine, as can be seen from his writings. Since, according to the holy Fathers, there is no necessity in this matter but rather a free choice, they did not separate from Augustine over this or quarrel with him. Therefore, it would also be commendable today if the opposing side would abandon this unnecessary dispute.

11. Why do you speak so much about Augustine, who actually agrees with the Zwinglians? In the Questions on the Old and New Testaments, *four commandments are counted in the first tablet.*

The correct answer to this is: Although this book is attributed to Augustine, the critical review and considerations provided for this book indicate, with convincing reasons, that this book is not actually by Augustine.* In his genuine, acknowledged writings, Augustine aligns entirely with us. For example, in *Against Faustus the Manichaean,* Book 15, Chapter 7, he writes: "The second commandment is, 'You shall not take the name of the Lord your God in vain'; the third concerns the rest of the Sabbath. Seven pertain to the love of neighbor."

The same, *On the Ten Chords,* chapters 5 and 6: "The Ten Commandments are here distributed so that three pertain to God and seven to men. Thus, the third commandment concerns the Sabbath. The first group has three cords; the second has seven. This series of seven begins with the honor of parents."

This excellent teacher, Augustine, has addressed in detail the question that lies between us and the Calvinists, and has nearly resolved it in advance with careful deliberation. In *Question 17, on Exodus,* he discusses the following:

> It is asked how the Ten Commandments should be divided: whether there are four up to the commandment on the Sabbath, which pertain to God, and then six that per-

* Modern scholarship agrees with Martini, attributing the work to "Ambrosiaster," an anonymous writer of the 4th century.

tain to human matters, the first of which is "Honor your father and mother"; or whether instead there are three and then seven. For those who say there are four separate the statement, "You shall have no other gods before me," so that "You shall not make for yourself a carved image" becomes a separate commandment, prohibiting worship of any likeness or image. They also wish to make "You shall not covet your neighbor's wife" and "You shall not covet your neighbor's house" into a single commandment, extending to the end.

However, those who count three in the first table and seven in the second hold that everything about worshiping one God is a single commandment: that nothing else should be honored as God besides Him. They divide the last commandments into two, so that "You shall not covet your neighbor's wife" is one commandment, and "You shall not covet your neighbor's house, servant, etc." is another. Neither group doubts that there are ten commandments in total, as the Scripture testifies.

Yet, to me, it seems more fitting to consider them as three in the first table and seven in the second, since the three pertaining to God appear to reflect the Trinity to those who study carefully. Indeed, the statement "You shall have no other gods before Me" is more fully explained when the worship of images is prohibited.

In this passage, Augustine argues that the desire for a neighbor's wife and for any other possession can each be counted separately: "You shall not covet your neighbor's wife" and "You shall not covet your neighbor's house."

Since it can be observed that those who speak of God reveal the Trinity when carefully considered—and indeed, as it is said, "You shall have no other gods before me"—this is fully clarified by the prohibition against honoring images.

Shortly thereafter, he states, "I hold that God has distinguished the desire for a neighbor's wife from the desire for other things, since both commandments begin with 'You shall not covet your neighbor's wife,' and then it goes on to list other things."

Likewise, in *Confessions*, Book 3, Chapter 8: "One lives wrongly against the three and the seven, against the Psalter of ten strings, against Your Decalogue, O God, most high and most sweet."

He also repeats this in *Sermon 95, de Tempore.*

Thus, our division is supported by the foremost teacher among all the Fathers, Augustine, and it is clearly evident that he did not view it as something new, since it was already present and in use in the Church of God during his time and earlier. From that time on, the teachers of the Christian Church have followed this division of the Ten Commandments as taught by Augustine, while leaving aside the other arrangement. This is evident from Peter Lombard in *Sentences*, Book 3, Distinction 37; Bede in *On the Psalter*, his *Commentary on the Epistle to the Romans;* Bernard in *On Conscience*; Nicholas of Lyra on *Exodus*, chapter 20; Hugh in *Questions*, Article 4; and the *Glossa Ordinaria*.

It is worth noting that these teachers, who lived after Augustine's time, attributed the division followed by the Calvinists to Origen, as did Peter Lombard, Hugh of Saint-Cher*, and Thomas Aquinas, while they attributed our division to Augustine. Now, Origen, who was a controversial figure, cannot be compared in authority or standing, nor in judgment and understanding of divine matters, with the holy and renowned teacher Augustine, who shone like a bright light in the true Church of God.

---

* Hugh of Saint-Cher (1200–1263), although not as well-remembered today as Lombard and Aquinas, was once prominent among the Dominican Scholastic theologians.

12. You previously mentioned that dividing the Ten Commandments belongs to things of indifference. If that is true, why is it not considered indifferent to count exactly ten commandments, no more and no less? Likewise, why is it necessary to place them in two tables?

Where God's Word speaks explicitly, that is not a matter of indifference. There it says, "You shall not add to it; you shall not take away from it." In the specific enumeration of the Ten Commandments, I find no word or trace indicating that it must necessarily be held in a particular way, as is shown. But that I count Ten Commandments, no more and no less, and that I place them necessarily in two tables—this is God's arrangement and the course of His Word, which one rightly follows. For God Himself counts ten commandments in Exodus 34, where the Septuagint translators call them Δέκα λόγους (the "Ten Words"), as in Deuteronomy 4. Likewise, they are set on two tablets in Exodus 31 and 32, as well as in Deuteronomy 4 and 5. They are also enumerated by the Lord Christ Himself in Matthew 22.

13. Can one dispute the matter as one wishes, but doesn't Luther's division still omit the commandment on images?

Nothing is omitted in its meaning. The commandment "You shall have no other gods before me" encompasses all those other words within it. For whoever has no foreign gods and bears an abhorrence for all kinds of idolatry will also not worship idols. Luther omitted those words, as well as some others, so that he could present the Ten Commandments to the common people in a concise tablet, summarizing them in ten words.

14. Since it is written in Exodus 20, "You shall not make for yourself a carved image or any likeness," is it therefore asked in vain whether the Lutherans do right by tolerating and allowing images in their churches?

Here one must first carefully learn to distinguish between images and idols. For although both, in terms of outward appearance, form, and shape, may simply be images made of wood, metal, stone, or similar materials, they differ in usage. Some images are turned into idols and forbidden by God. Thus, images that are worshiped and venerated as divine become idols and objects of idolatry for their worshipers and venerated; however, for those who do not worship or revere them as divine, they are neither idols nor objects of idolatry.

Therefore, since this commandment speaks only of idol images, it should be noted that it does not prohibit images tolerated in Lutheran churches. It is plainly evident that no idol or object of idolatry is allowed in Lutheran churches, and it is well known that, through blessed Martin Luther, idols and images of idolatry were removed and abolished from Lutheran churches so thoroughly that they have not been permitted up to the present time.

15. But how will you prove that this commandment does not abolish images in Lutheran churches, since the reason you have given does not satisfy me?

I can prove this with irrefutable arguments. First, one must consider the Hebrew language, in which God wrote and gave this law, where we find the two words *Pesel* and *Themuna*. These do not merely refer to idol images or images of idolatry but to all kinds of images, whether they are worshiped as divine or not. They encompass everything perceived by the senses or conceived in thought, or made by the hands of an artist, painted, carved, or sculpted. It would then follow that God's Law would destroy and overturn nature itself, as will soon be further explained.

16. Even though I place this in its proper context, am I still not somewhat troubled that it says specifically here, "You shall not make for yourself any likeness, etc.; do not worship them," and not simply, *"You shall not make any image to worship it"?*

Although the matter is sufficiently clear, we can still provide additional, tangible arguments to support our position. In Leviticus 26, the Lord speaks and clarifies Himself as follows: "You shall not set up for yourselves a carved pillar or place a figured stone in your land to worship it, for I am the Lord your God." This is certainly clear enough.

Again, in Deuteronomy 4, the Lord repeats this command in the following manner: "You saw no form on the day the Lord spoke to you from the fire on Mount Horeb, so that you do not corrupt yourselves by making for yourselves any image in the form of a man or woman, or any animal on the earth, or any bird under the sky, or any creature that moves on the ground, or any fish in the waters below the earth. And do not lift your eyes to the heavens and see the sun, the moon, the stars—all the host of heaven—and be drawn away to worship and serve them."

Nowhere in the aforementioned words is there any set restriction to choose as they please. They must either agree with us that such images of animals, birds, reptiles, fish, and stars are prohibited only *in respect to purpose and end*—that they must not be worshiped, as Moses himself clarifies when he sets this condition and explicitly mentions it in Leviticus; and thus, their [that is, the Calvinists'] teaching about iconoclasm is false. Or, if they wish to assert that the images mentioned are simply forbidden *without any condition,* whether they are worshiped or not, then it would remain eternally true that no one could depict even a sheep or a goat, not even a sparrow or a grasshopper, as animals, birds, and fish are so clearly mentioned. Moreover, no one could have one's likeness painted as a man or woman, since the form of man or woman is also explicitly referred to here. And just as Hezekiah imposed a particular moral law in one instance, so would such images be prohibited either within the church or outside of it, whether in books, coats of arms, seals, or elsewhere.

In such a case, the Roman Emperor's eagle, the Palatinate lion of the Electors, the lion of the Dutch, the harpy of the County of East Frisia, and our three stars of the North would all vanish from their places and be extinguished. Indeed, all coins would have to disappear as well. For the commandment contains no such exception, allowing images to be prohibited in the church but permitted on the coats of arms of secular rulers or on coins, etc. I find no such exception in Moses. Even what might seem plausible here, based on God's prohibition regarding images, is clearly given in Leviticus 19: "You shall not turn to idols or make for yourselves molten gods; for I am the LORD your God." Here, once again, this prohibition concerns foreign molten gods and is directed purely and solely at images that are worshiped, not at others.

17. Do you have more reasons to prove and support your view?

The second reason is this: If God the Lord had prohibited images entirely and not merely their misuse in the moral law, then it would follow that the moral law, which is founded on the single, enduring, and unchangeable will of God, would indeed contradict the Levitical ceremonial laws. The moral law does not change, as it reveals God's immutable will in His Ten Commandments, which He never alters. As shown in Scripture, it reflects God's rule consistently. Thus, I say, it would follow that this moral law would have to be in conflict with the Levitical church laws, which would mean that God's unchangeable will had been altered and was in opposition to itself. But this is impossible, for as God says through His mouth, "I am the Lord; I do not change."

Therefore, since God allowed images in the temple and in the royal house of Solomon, any reasonable Christian can conclude that the prohibition on images, as described, is founded on the unchangeable will of God and does not indiscriminately and without distinction condemn all images.

Thirdly, God the Lord permitted twelve bronze oxen to be made and placed under the great basin in the temple at Jerusalem. However, when the children of Israel erected a calf in the wilderness and worshiped it as divine, God the Lord, became angry and punished them for it.

Now the question is whether God the Lord, was angry simply because they had made and set up a calf. The correct answer is: No. For if He had disapproved of that kind of image in itself, He would not have allowed similar representations in the temple.

Fourthly, if in His law God the Lord had forbidden representation without the idolatrous misuse, He would not have portrayed and presented the cross of Christ to the Jewish people in the form of the bronze serpent in the wilderness. It is worth noting that this image remained among the Jewish people until they turned it into an idol. As soon as this misuse arose, God, following the rule of this commandment, ordered the serpent to be destroyed and crushed. Therefore, God could tolerate the image of the serpent itself, but He could not tolerate its misuse as an object of idolatry.

Fifthly, the image of our most holy altar, which many will maintain, teaches us through the example of the altar of the Reubenites. This altar was nothing other than an image and likeness of the altar of God that stood in the tabernacle, and at the same time, a reminder that they also belonged to the Lord. For they themselves declared before all Israel: "It was built so that in the future, when their children might speak to the other Israelites, their descendants, they could say: 'See this likeness of the altar of the Lord, which our fathers made—not for sacrifices or burnt offerings, etc.'" Thus, the altar of the Reubenites, according to their own confession, was an image and likeness of the true altar that stood in the tent of meeting, modeled after it and therefore called its likeness.

Sixthly, if God the Lord truly had an aversion and abhorrence for images—not merely due to the misuse but because of their form and physical likeness—then why would He Himself create such images? For all His bodily creatures have their own figures, forms, and images, as no one can deny.

Seventh, God the Lord Himself made the prophet Ezekiel into an artist, instructing him to depict the siege of Jerusalem on a clay tablet and to draw an army—clearly, these must have been human figures—and to portray the city in this way (Ezekiel 4).

Eighth, if all images are prohibited by the commandment against images in Exodus 20, and yet Moses, under this commandment, includes pillars and memorial stones within its explanation, as mentioned above in Leviticus 25, then no one today could justifiably erect even a single memorial stone or pillar any more than they could make images. Nor could even the most knowledgeable and pious believers avoid sinning against this commandment if they were to mark their boundaries with memorial stones or pillars.

Ninth, after the time of Solomon, the people of Israel were divided into two kingdoms: the Kingdom of Judah and the Kingdom of Israel. In both, places of worship were established, and images were set up. In the Kingdom of Israel was the temple in Jerusalem, where there were the twelve oxen, the lions, and the cherubim. In the Kingdom of Judah, there were also temples in Dan and Bethel, where calves were erected. If one considers the form, there is no difference between the oxen in the temple at Jerusalem and the calves at Bethel and Dan; indeed, there is as little difference as between the altar in Jerusalem and the altar of the Reubenites. Therefore, if God had hated the calves at Bethel and Dan because of their idolatrous form, then He would also have hated the oxen in the temple at Jerusalem and the altar of the Reubenites for the same reason. But He did not hate these, nor were they an abomination to Him. What is the reason for this? Clearly, as the prophets stated, the reason was that the calves in both places in the Kingdom of Israel were worshiped, while the oxen in the temple and the altar of the Reubenites were not worshiped.

Tenth, the history of the capture of the Ark of the Covenant by the Philistines clearly shows the undeniable distinction between the images prohibited in the Law of Moses and other images that were not prohibited. For when the Ark of the Lord was captured, it contained five golden mice and five golden images of their hind parts, according to the number of the five Philistine rulers—yet, idolatry was practiced with these items. In contrast, it could not tolerate an idolatrous image such as Dagon beside it, because he was worshiped by the Philistines as an idol.

Eleventh, the Apostle Paul says in Galatians 3, "O foolish Galatians, who has bewitched you, that you should not obey the truth, before whose eyes Jesus Christ was clearly portrayed?" And in Hebrews 10, "The Law, having only a shadow of the good things to come, and not the very image itself." These references are undeniably drawn from the art of painting to indicate that Christ, in the flesh, was presented in the Old Testament to the people of Israel as if through an outline or sketch that artists often use, until the true and substantial perfect image arrived and replaced the shadow of the Levitical law. For the Holy Spirit to compare the two Testaments, Old and New, which are so full of represented and foreshadowed goods, to something that God considers righteous, is something I cannot persuade myself to believe. Are not nearly all of God's revelations in Scripture full of images? How often does the Son of God appear in the form of a man, as in Genesis 18:22, Joshua

5, and elsewhere? Truly, anyone wishing to eliminate images would have to remove the entire Book of Revelation, for therein God shows His servant John everything through images and, as it were, paints before his eyes all that He wishes to reveal to him concerning the future state of His Church, as each chapter testifies.

Twelfth, the art of working with wood and stone, silver and gold, and of making various kinds of images, is practiced and praised as a special gift from God in the case of the renowned craftsmen Bezalel and Aholiab (Exodus 31), who also fashioned the two cherubim over the Ark of the Covenant (Exodus 37). Similarly, the Holy Spirit praises the craftsman Hiram, who, besides producing various works for the temple, also made the twelve oxen on which the cast sea stood. This art was not newly learned by him, but had been practiced long before, such that when Solomon saw fit, he summoned Hiram from a foreign land because of his renowned skill, to direct our craftsmen in Israel (1 Kings 7).

We present these twelve reasons for every devout Christian to consider carefully and reflect upon.

18. What, then, is to be said about the depiction of the Heavenly Father in the form of an old man with a gray head and beard—is this contrary to divine truth?

To this, we rightly respond that we do not indiscriminately or recklessly approve of every image of God the Father or of the Holy Trinity. Nevertheless, if it were entirely wrong to depict God the Father, and especially for the reason that His image as an old man with a gray head is supposedly contrary to truth, then the holy prophet Daniel would be implicated in this. For he describes God the Father, before whom God the Son, appearing like a man, is brought in the clouds of heaven, using precisely such an image, with these exact words. It is written, "The Ancient of Days took His seat; His clothing was white as snow, and the hair of His head like wool." Thus, God the Father Himself wished to reveal Himself in such an image and in the form of an old man with gray hair—not with the idea that in His own divine, eternal essence He is truly an old gray-haired man like us men, but rather, through this image, to symbolically portray His eternal majesty and to signify that He is the first and the last, existing from eternity, outside of all time.

In similar form, He also appeared to the prophet Isaiah, "on a high and lofty throne, and the train of His robe filled the temple" (Isaiah 6).

The question here is whether one may depict this revelation and vision in a painting.

We answer: Yes. For if it can be described and depicted with words, why should it not also be portrayed in lineaments? Since our understanding can barely grasp the image, such a visual portrayal brings the concept to life for us. And indeed, the Zwinglians argue that it is entirely impermissible to paint any image of God, regardless of the intent or purpose, to such an extent that even the forms of revelation—where God the Father appeared as just described, the Son in assumed flesh, and the Holy Spirit in the form of a dove—should supposedly be forbidden to depict even in a historical manner.

We would gladly hear how they would justify their illustrations that aim to represent divinity. For it is consistently and indisputably true that in some Calvinist places, Bibles are adorned with such images, wherein not only is the great name of God (*Jehovah*) written in Hebrew letters, but also depicted with a surrounding glow, similar to the radiance of the sun or the brightness of heaven. However, the commandment in Exodus 20 and Deuteronomy 4 expressly forbids us from making any image resembling a man (interpreted to mean representing His divine, incomprehensible essence), and also from creating images and likenesses of anything in heaven above (thus also including the sun along with its rays and the brightness of heaven). Therefore, they strike themselves with their own sword.

19. But what do you want to answer regarding the passages in Isaiah 40: "To whom will you liken God? Or what likeness will you compare to Him?" and in Romans 1: "They have exchanged the glory of the immortal God for an image made to look like a mortal human being"?

If the passage from Isaiah were to prohibit our images, it would also prohibit the Calvinists' depictions. But it should be noted that the second passage does not contradict the indicated apparitions and manifestations of God, in which He appears in a human manner to the prophets. For the Holy Spirit is here preaching about the pagans, who are entirely ensnared in distorted error and blindness, as if God in His own divine essence were like a human being, with eyes and ears, etc.—just as they imagine about their god Jupiter, who, according to their myths, interacted with human women and fathered children with them. In this heathen delusion, they erect images of their pagan gods, worship them, and revere them as divine. Against this, the prophet Isaiah speaks and says: "To whom will you liken God? Or what likeness will you compare to Him?"

As Saint Paul's testimony further confirms, it should not be concluded, either from the prophet Isaiah's or Saint Paul's words, that they strictly forbid such depictions. If one insists on this interpretation, then it would have to be unavoidably asserted that Isaiah contradicts the prophet Daniel, or even himself in his own sixth chapter.

20. What, then, should one think of the crucifix and other depictions of the Passion? Should they, too, be driven out of the church?

As for the crucifix, in its proper use—when it is used as a reminder of the suffering and death of Jesus Christ—it can well be tolerated in the Church, and should never be misused. For if it were so offensive to God to recall the Passion in images, why did He Himself choose to depict Christ's suffering and crucifixion through a bronze serpent raised on a pole, as if painted before the eyes of His people? This is shown in the account in Numbers 21 and in the Lord Christ's interpretation in John 3. Although this was meant as a particular type, nonetheless it reveals that the Divine Majesty does not object to the depiction of Christ's Passion in and of itself, and that one can, without sin, recall Christ's suffering through figures and images.

Who would object today if someone looked at a pelican, whether alive or depicted in an image, nourishing its young with blood flowing from its opened breast, and was reminded of how Christ, with blood flowing from His opened side, nourishes us unto eternal life? As Saint Augustine also reflects on this in his commentary on Psalm 101.

21. Is it still questionable whether one may paint a pelican?

Some of the Zwinglians agree with us [i.e., that it is permissible], answering: "Yes"; others oppose us, answering: "No." If they say "no," then it is clear that they condemn the entire art of painting, for then one would not be allowed to depict even a bird or a pelican. In this way, all Christians would be sorely disturbed by what the Zwinglians prohibit and insist upon. But if they say "yes," it is permitted, then we further ask whether one could, with a clear conscience, consider the blood of Christ and its power when viewing such a painted pelican with its young? If they answer yes, then their arguments and beliefs are unfounded and are simply an idea of their own, where they belong. But if they answer "no," then we leave it to the judgment of the whole Christian Church to determine what to make of such teachers and their doctrine, and what kind of tyranny they are attempting to introduce into Christendom by trying to impose human commandments on people's consciences regarding things that Christ Himself has left free.

Moreover, the Zwinglians surely do not disagree that, when the cross of Christ is mentioned in a sermon, its image is immediately awakened in the minds of both the preacher and the listeners. Indeed, it is impossible to think of the cross of Christ without such an image forming in the mind. Thus, if the iconoclasts' arguments were to hold any weight, they would also have to reform their own imagination and thoughts.

Moreover, the best preachers are considered to be those (as the Apostle clearly indicates in Galatians 3) who can preach about the crucified Christ in such a way that they vividly portray Him to the listeners, as if they were seeing Him hanging on the cross before them. All of this would be lost under the opposing view.

22. How can one accurately paint Christ on the cross or His apostles, given that no one now living in the world has seen them? This could never truly be done. Thus, would not falsehood be strengthened both against the first and second tables of the Ten Commandments of God, bearing false witness both against the Creator and His creation?

This external objection is one the Zwinglians have also raised. Regarding the first table, it has already been adequately explained that images of Christ and His apostles, outside the context of idolatrous worship, are not in opposition to the commandment. Now, as for the second table, dear reader, consider the argument which these individuals present: They claim that if an image does not perfectly capture a person, it constitutes false witness against the second table of the Ten Commandments. For even though it is impossible to portray with accuracy those whom no one now living has seen, they maintain that all images which do not perfectly resemble their subjects are false witnesses against the second table.

If this were true, then all images created by painters in training, who initially struggle to capture likenesses accurately, would be considered nothing but pure falsehood and thus a violation of God's Law. Consequently, many would also condemn goldsmiths, minters, carvers, printers with their woodcuts, tapestry makers, locksmiths with their engraved keys, furniture makers, decorative painters, honeycomb engravers, and many other artists and craftsmen. For if their images do not perfectly match the originals, they, too, would be guilty of bearing false witness against the second table of the Ten Commandments.

Jacobus Francus* in his *Relatione Historica* and our neighboring Dutch would also be equally guilty if they portray battles, sieges, victories, and triumphs in paintings or engrave them artistically in copper. For where no one's likeness, much less that of a single lancer or soldier, is depicted accurately, then, by their reasoning, we would have to seek out exactness and accuse them of bearing false witness, which would be an uncharitable misuse [of the commandment] and indeed sinful. Following this logic, every time we think of Adam and Eve, Enoch, Noah, Shem, Abraham, Isaac, Jacob, Moses, Aaron, Elijah, Elisha, and other prophets of God, or even Christ Himself—and as it often happens, when we imagine them in our minds (since no thought occurs without images, as has now been pointed out)—all such images would then constitute false witness. And, since no one living today has ever seen them, no one could imagine their true likeness. Consequently, to avoid

---

* Jacobus Francus was the pseudonym of Conrad Lautenbach (1534–95) whose most renowned work was posthumously published as *Historicae Relationis Continuatio* (1598). It was the compilation of works he had written twice a year for the Frankfurt book fair, as an ongoing record of contemporary history, combined with maps and plates.

so many false testimonies, we should never think of Adam or Abraham, Jacob, the prophets, or even Christ Himself.

These, then, are the supposed substantial arguments of the Calvinists against images in Christ's churches. And whatever we have argued regarding images thus far, we intend also to apply to the other *adiaphora* (matters of indifference) commonly used and understood in the churches of the Augsburg Confession.

23. I am satisfied with the explanation regarding images. Tell me further, what is the general virtue of the first table?

The fear of God.

24. What is the fear of God?

The fear of God is when one acknowledges the true, living God—as He has revealed Himself in His Church: God the Father, Son, and Holy Spirit—according to the doctrine given by Him. It involves a heartfelt fear of His great wrath against sin, while also believing that, for Christ's sake, sins are forgiven and that we have a gracious God. This faith is sealed by the Holy Sacraments instituted by the Lord Christ, and we, illuminated by this faith, call upon Him and honor Him through good works, which He desires and has commanded to be done. We also avoid all sins that are contrary to God, with the purpose that the Lord God may be praised and honored in us.

25. You say I should honor God with good works: Are good works then a service to God necessary for salvation?

Not at all, since we are saved by grace through faith and not by works, as stated in Ephesians 2.

26. What purpose do good works serve?

While we do not attribute to good works the power to save, nonetheless there are other reasons that motivate the godly to diligently practice good works. These reasons partly regard God Himself and partly our neighbor. As for the Lord God, it is evident that His honor is greatly spread through our good works, for He Himself testifies that He is honored by them (Matthew 5; Romans 12; Colossians 1; Philippians 1; 1 Peter 2; 1 Timothy 6).

Then, the reasons for performing good works with regard to people are twofold: either for our own sake or for the sake of our neighbor. For the sake of our neighbor, it is to demonstrate our faith to them, for faith without works is dead (James 2). Additionally, we show our Christian love toward them. Moreover, we do good works to fulfill our Christian calling and confession (Ephesians 2; 2 Peter 1); to avoid punishment (1 Corinthians 6; Galatians 6); and finally, to enjoy the blessings with which the Lord God is accustomed to reward the works of the godly.

27. So I understand that the Lord God indeed rewards good works?

Yes, certainly. The Lord God has set a great reward upon good works, which is twofold: temporal rewards in this life and the promise of eternal life in the life to come (1 Timothy 4).

In this temporal life, those who live according to God's Law are provided with riches, good health, and long life (Deuteronomy 28; Proverbs 10; Ezekiel 20; Ephesians 6; Psalms 41, 128). In eternal life, they will be bestowed with great honor and glory, named among the godly (Matthew 25; 1 Corinthians 15)—a glory that no person can fully comprehend or know (Isaiah 64; 1 Corinthians 2).

28. Where does this reward come from? Does it come from merit?

No. It does not come from merit or from the power of good works but from God's goodness, grace, and mercy, for He has promised it and attached it to good works.

29. What is the chief virtue of the second table?

Love of neighbor.

30. What is the love of neighbor?

Love of neighbor is a movement of the heart by which we love our neighbor as ourselves, desire, wish, and offer all good things to them, and, according to our station, help, encourage, and support them in every need. We seek their well-being in all things, do good before them, and turn all things to their benefit. All this is done so that God's name may be honored and the holy Christian Church may be planted and spread far and wide.

31. What good works flow primarily from this virtue?

The love of parents, children, teachers, authorities, and the like; also mercy, kindness, goodness, gentleness, unity, friendship, humility, justice, marital love, fairness in all kinds of contracts, mildness, sincerity, faithfulness, truthfulness, and avoidance of meddling, slander, betrayal, and similar actions.

The Apostle Paul writes beautifully on this in 1 Corinthians 13, saying: "Love is patient and kind; love does not envy; love does not boast or act pridefully; it is not easily angered; it keeps no record of wrongs; it does not rejoice in wrongdoing but rejoices in the truth. It bears all things, believes all things, hopes all things, and never fails," etc.

32. Can you not give me a general description or definition of the Law of God?

Yes, indeed: The Law of God is the eternal and unchangeable wisdom and rule of justice in God, which distinguishes right and wrong, good and evil, and terribly condemns all and every kind of disobedience that conflicts with this rule, which is in God and has been revealed to humanity in creation, and subsequently often repeated and clarified by the mouth of God, so that we may know that there is one God, our Creator, who binds all rational creatures and demands that they conform to Him, and condemns and destroys all who are not conformed to Him, unless forgiveness of sins and reconciliation with God occur through Christ, our Mediator.

33. *What purpose does the Law of God serve for me, and what benefit does its daily contemplation provide?*

Firstly, the knowledge of the Law of God is a certain testimony that there truly exists a true and living God.

Secondly, it teaches also *qualis sit Deus* (what God is), namely, righteous and true, and how the Law portrays Him.

Thirdly, it teaches the purpose of human creation; namely, that men may know God and live obediently to Him according to His Law.

Fourthly, it reveals sin and its eternal judgment and the justice of God, which condemns and accuses all people who do not seek refuge in the Lord Christ, our Mediator.

Fifthly, it is a rule for good works, according to which the reborn should practice their obedience toward God.

Sixthly, it is a norm for human life, even for those who are not reborn, that they may regulate their conduct through honest discipline and correction.

34. *Can a person then fulfill the Law of God?*

No person in this corrupted nature can render perfect obedience to the Law of God (Rom. 7:8). However, outward conduct can be regulated according to it, even by those who are not reborn.

35. *Did the Lord Christ fulfill the Law of God?*

Certainly, and He did so in multiple ways:

(1) By upholding and demonstrating perfect obedience Himself.

(2) By atoning for and paying the debt that we incurred

through our transgression and disobedience.

(3) By teaching and explaining the true and correct understanding of the Law.

(4) And finally, by awakening in the hearts of believers a new obedience conformable to the Law, through the Holy Spirit.

36. I understand that through the merit of Christ we are redeemed from the Law. Likewise, we read in 1 Timothy: "The law is not given for the righteous," and also in Romans 6: "We are not under the law, but under grace." What, then, does the law grant us?

It is true that those who are justified through faith in the Son of God are also redeemed from the Law in terms of its condemnation and obligation to eternal punishment and suffering. Nevertheless, the eternal and unchangeable obligation to obedience remains. For as Christ took upon Himself the curse of the Law, He thereby renewed human nature and reestablished obedience or conformity with the Law of God. For Christ did not come to abolish the Law, but to fulfill it. From this, it is easy to understand what Christian freedom is and how far it extends.

37. What is Christian freedom, then?

Christian freedom is not a freedom by which one may do whatever one wishes; rather, it is liberation, redemption, and deliverance from sin, from the wrath of God, from the curse of the Law, from Jewish ceremonies, from Mosaic civil ordinances, and from all manner of human regulations and intermediate matters without offense. (John 8; Romans 6, 7, 8; Ephesians 2; Galatians 3, 4, 5.)

On Sin.

38. I understand that through the Law of God, sin is recognized, imputed, and condemned; therefore, instruct me further, what, then, is sin or what is it called?

To speak briefly: Sin is everything that conflicts with the Law of God (1 John 3). Or sin is a lack or omission, or action, conflicting with the Law of God, and deserving the wrath of God, eternal punishments, unless it is forgiven for Christ's sake.

39. Who is the first cause of sin?

The cause of sin is not God the Lord, as is very improperly taught by the Zwinglians; but rather the free will of the devil and of men, who have voluntarily turned away from God the Lord and have lost the wisdom, righteousness, and also the freedom of will, which were implanted in them at creation, for themselves and for their entire posterity and descendants.

40. You say the Zwinglians make God the cause of sin, and I would like to hear that reported from their own writings?

Yes, they teach openly that God the Lord is the cause of sin, and that He has also decided so in His eternal counsel, that man should sin. For thus writes Calvin in *lib. 3. Inst. cap. 23. v. 7:* "I ask, whence comes it, that Adam's fall makes so many nations with their underage children subject to eternal death: It is because it pleased God so." I must confess, that this is a dreadful counsel. But yet, no one can deny that God permitted it and that He knew it beforehand. But Calvin maintains: "For He had *arranged* it thus in His counsel." Furthermore, he says at this place, that it is a cold, empty notion, a cold gesture, if anyone praises it: "*decretum fuisse a Deo, ut sua defectione periret homo*" ("It was decreed by God that man would perish through his own fall"). Likewise, in his commentary on the first book of Moses, *cap. 3. pag. 26,* Calvin writes that God gave the devil the tongue as a sword again to misuse it as a tool to deceive mankind—not otherwise than if a murderer were given a sword in his hand to strike a fatal blow with it. Théodorus Beza *coll. Mump. lat. pag. 526. 527.* says: "Adam and Eve had to sin because God had decided it so in His eternal counsel."

Zanchius, *lib. 3. de natura Dei cap. 4. fol. 331.* says: "*Consentium nihil in mundo fieri invito Deo, nec peccatum originale, sapientissimo Dei consilio.*" — "Nothing happens in the world against God's will, nor does original sin enter the world without the most wise counsel of God." Also, *lib. 5. cap. 2. fol. 677. Th. 3.*: "*Non falso dicitur, universos homines eo fuisse Ordinatos, ut permitterentur peccare.*" — "It is not wrongly said that all men were appointed by God to be allowed to sin."

41. Why do you want to prove that this doctrine is false?

Because this is contrary to God and His holy Word, it becomes the fiercest controversy, and the following points are diligently learned. David says, Psalm 5: "You are not a God to whom wickedness is pleasing; the wicked will not stand before You." Hosea 13: "You bring yourself into misfortune, for your fate is only with God." John 3: "Whoever commits sin is of the devil, for the devil has sinned from the beginning" John 8: "The devil has not stood in the truth, because he is a liar and the father of it." And in Ezekiel, the Lord says: "As surely as I live, I do not desire the death of the wicked, but that he turn from his ways" (Ezekiel 33). And indeed, we know that God the Lord gave His Law for this reason, that it should be His rule, His holy, unchanging will, by which we should not only recognize our sin, but also understand how severely God has forbidden sin, and how sharply He intended to punish it, both here temporally and there eternally, unless it is completely avoided by human beings, or again, forgiven through true repentance. If God earnestly forbids sin and also desires to punish it, how can it be said that He wills it, or that He is its cause? Or how can it be said, as Zanchius blasphemously writes (lib. 3 *De Natura Dei*, cap. 4, pag. 34), *quod neque voluntas Dei sit absoluta, ut praecepta servent & promissiones assequantur impii*—"It is not God's perfect will for the ungodly to keep His commandments and receive His promises."

Does this mean that God the Lord assigns two contradictory wills? It is indeed true that hardening of the heart is ascribed in Holy Scripture, in one place, to God the Lord; in another, to the devil; and in a third, to mankind. As in Exodus 4: "But I will harden Pharaoh's heart, so that he will not let the people go." Isaiah 6: "Harden the heart of this people, and make their ears heavy, and blind their eyes," etc. Exodus 8 and 9: "But Pharaoh hardened his heart." 2 Chronicles 26: "Zedekiah was stiff-necked and hardened his heart." 2 Kings 17; Zechariah 7: "They hardened their hearts," etc. 2 Corinthians 4: "If our gospel is veiled, it is veiled to those who are perishing, in whom the god of this world has blinded the minds of the unbelievers, so that they cannot see the light of the glorious gospel."

When, therefore, this same and singular effect—namely hardening and blindness—is not simultaneously attributed in the same respect (*eodem respectu*) to these three causes—God, man, and the devil, which are as far apart as heaven, earth, and hell—one must here learn from God's Word to make such a distinction in causation so that the Lord God is excluded from the efficient causes of sins. Therefore, one must understand that God hardens and blinds the ungodly when, as a righteous Judge, and on account of their contempt for His Word and other grave sins, He withdraws His gracious hand and does not grant them grace for conversion. Instead, He gives them over to their own flesh, all their evil desires, and even to the devil himself, into ruin. We have an example of this in Pharaoh (Exodus 9; Romans 9). This is also explained in Psalm 81: "But My people did not listen to my voice, and Israel would not submit to me. So I let them go in the stubbornness of their hearts, that they might walk according to their own counsel." Thus, the hardening is attributed to God the Lord as a punishment for preceding sins, which in itself is a righteous work of God's justice. For when God the Lord withdraws His hand in such a way and gives the godless over, they fall into the power of the devil, who then works in the children of unbelief (Eph. 2). He drives them with force to rush toward hell, and at that point, no punishment or warning is of any help; rather, they become more and more hardened with each passing day. And because the human heart was already harder than a rock and their understanding blind to divine matters due to their inborn corruption, this is then compounded by delusion and the devil's influence so that the hope of their conversion becomes rare.

If, then, the corruption is, as far as it is a sin, really a work of the devil, it is also the work of the human being himself, as can clearly be seen from the testimonies we have set forth. Whoever diligently observes this distinction will easily guard himself against the perilous disputation of the opposite view.

42. But the Calvinists today do not want to admit that they have ever made God the cause of sin, or that they still do so?

It is true. They protest today very strongly against it. But with this, they defend and excuse their forefathers in no way. They whisper and turn the matter here and there. One wants to interpret it in the way of Calvin, Beza. Another wants to interpret it differently. But it does not help them, no matter how they turn, or try to embellish, because the word is clear, and it is often repeated in the same way. Therefore, if today's Calvinist writers do not want to be called blasphemous in the same way, they must face the matter rightly, publicly condemn this teaching, and separate themselves from Calvin, Beza, and others publicly. Then they would be excused before God and men. But as long as they seek to cloak and embellish such grave errors, they make themselves complicit in them and fall ever deeper into them along with those errors.

The Second Part
Concerning Christian Faith.

Genesis 15:6.

"Abraham believed the Lord, and He counted it to him as righteousness."

John 3.

"For God so loved the world that He gave His only begotten Son, that whoever believes in Him should not perish but have eternal life."

Romans 1.

"The Gospel is the power of God to bring salvation to everyone who believes."

1. *How many articles are there in the Christian faith?*

Three, which are also otherwise divided into twelve.*

2. *What does the First Article concern?*

Creation.

3. *How is it stated?*

"I believe in God the Father Almighty, Maker of heaven and earth."

What does this mean?

Answer: I believe that God has created me, along with all creatures; that He has given me body and soul, eyes, ears, and all limbs, reason, and all the senses, and still sustains them;

* Martini refers here to the Papist tradition of dividing the creed into twelve articles—one for each apostle.

that He also provides me with clothing and shoes, food and drink, house and home, spouse and children, fields, livestock, and all goods, and richly and daily supplies all that I need to support this body and life; protects me against all danger; and guards and keeps me from all evil. And all this out of pure, fatherly, divine goodness and mercy, without any merit or worthiness in me. For all this I am bound to thank, praise, serve, and obey Him. This is most certainly true.

4. What does the Second Article concern?

Redemption.

5. How is it stated?

And in Jesus Christ, His only Son, our Lord, who was conceived by the Holy Spirit, born of the Virgin Mary, suffered under Pontius Pilate, was crucified, died, and was buried, descended into hell; on the third day, rose again from the dead; ascended into heaven, sits at the right hand of God the Almighty Father, from where He will come to judge the living and the dead.

What does this mean?

Answer: I believe that Jesus Christ, true God, begotten of the Father from eternity, and also true man, born of the Virgin Mary, is my Lord, who has redeemed me, a lost and condemned person, purchased and won me from all sins, from death, and from the power of the devil, not with gold or silver, but with His holy, precious blood, and with His innocent suffering and death; that I may be His own, live under Him in His kingdom, and serve Him in everlasting righteousness, innocence, and blessedness, just as He is risen from the dead, lives and reigns to all eternity. This is most certainly true.

6. What does the Third Article concern?

Sanctification.

7. How is it stated?

I believe in the Holy Spirit, one holy Christian Church, the communion of saints, the forgiveness of sins, the resurrection of the body, and eternal life. Amen.

What does this mean?

Answer: I believe that I cannot by my own reason or strength believe in Jesus Christ, my Lord, or come to Him, but the Holy Spirit has called me through the Gospel, enlightened me with His gifts, sanctified and kept me in the true faith. Just as He calls, gathers, enlightens, sanctifies, and keeps the whole of Christendom on earth with Jesus Christ in the one true faith. In this Christian Church, He daily and abundantly forgives all my sins and the sins of all believers, and on the Last Day will raise me and all the dead, and will grant me and all believers in Christ eternal life. – This is most certainly true.

8. If one applies these Articles of the Christian Faith to the Law, it seems that one might be able to know the description of God's essence as revealed in the holy Word. Therefore, tell me, what is God?

He is a single, indivisible, unfathomable spiritual being; eternal, infinite, true, righteous, merciful, almighty; the eternal Father, and the Son, the image of the Father, and the Holy Spirit, who proceeds from the Father and the Son. He has revealed Himself in the creation of the world and in His Word, which He has given to His Church, and according to which He wishes to be known, honored, and celebrated and praised by all people alone in all eternity.

9. Do the Zwinglians fully agree with this definition?

Not entirely. For they teach that in nature there are things God is unable to do or to alter according to His will, and thus they contend against the divine omnipotence. Thus, Peter

Martyr responds in his *Dialogues* to Brentz's statement (that Christ's body cannot accomplish something on its own but is enabled to do so through God's power and might) with the following words: *Ego vero contra tibi affirmo Nulla Vi, fieri Posse, ut res creata sit ubique.* That is, "On the contrary, I say that no power or force can make a created thing be everywhere." And our opponents have gathered many such Calvinistic statements in their writings.*

10. The Calvinists write thus, but claim that it does not necessarily follow that even if they say something is impossible for God and His power they must thereby deny His omnipotence.

But what else would follow, dear Christian? For when one says, "Something is impossible for God and His omnipotence," they are also saying that God cannot do something. Whoever says this is also saying that God cannot do everything. Now, it follows indisputably that whoever says, "God cannot do everything," is saying that God's power is not so capable or mighty that it can do all things. If it is unable in some respect, then it is a lack of power; if it lacks power in something, then it is powerless in that area. And if it is powerless in any respect, then it is not omnipotent.

11. This discourse seems as though it may not be based on solid grounds. For first, Paul and the early Church Fathers also explicitly mention certain things that God cannot do, such as lie, die, or sin. Yet they do not deny God's power for this reason. Samothenes, Calvin, Martyr, Beza, and others write that when they say God cannot do

---

* What is under contention is the Scriptural teaching set forth by Lutherans such as Johannes Brenz (1499–1570) which is called the "ubiquity doctrine," which explains that Christ Jesus is present in all places according to both His divine and human natures—the human nature being so present because of the communication of attributes. The Calvinists maintained that such a presence is "impossible" for the human nature.

this or that, they commonly add salvâ et incólumi ipsius potestate, *that is, "without any detriment to His divine power." How, then, can one say that they deny the omnipotence of God? And further, when Calvinist writers mention certain things that are impossible for God to do, they are referring to things that are contrary to God's eternal truth and nature. Now, Lutherans themselves must admit that God cannot do what contradicts His own nature. Therefore, they must either deny God's omnipotence themselves, or else recognize the Calvinist writers as being right and just in this regard.*

This discourse of ours is correct and certainly rests on its immovable foundations, such that it is not moved in the least by these objections. Before we respond to them, however, we must first inform the Christian reader a bit about the terms of this question. First of all, it should be noted that the word *potentia* (power), from which the word *omnipotentia* (omnipotence) is derived, is used in two ways: actively and passively; that is, by such *potentiam,* one either acts or suffers. (Arist. *lib.* 8. *Metaph. t.* 7. *l.* 6. Arist. *de anim. t.* 6.) This distinction, however, is such that *potentia* is not equally called active and passive, since the word *potentia* truly or properly means "power" πρὸς ἕν καὶ ἀφ' ἑνὸς [toward one and from one]. And thus, *potentia* refers, properly speaking, only to a capacity of force through which one accomplishes and executes something actively. Subsequently, however, as secondary and with respect to active *potentia,* passive *potentia* is also called *potentia,* a power or ability (*posse*), which otherwise is more properly called ἀδυναμία [lack of power or impotence], meaning an impotence, and does not consist in action and power but rather in suffering or passive endurance. As can be seen in Philo, marg. C. 8, where he divides the second type of quality into *potentiam* and *impotentiam* and does not deny that, as also is shown by Greek and Latin interpreters, *certo modo* and *respectu* under *potentia* is included *impotentia sive* ἀδυναμία [impotence or inability].

If this is taken into consideration and properly examined, it is very easy to respond to the referenced passages. When, for example, the Apostle writes that God cannot lie (Hebrews 6:18) or that He cannot deny Himself (2 Timothy 2), or when James writes that God cannot sin, etc., we see that in the first passage from Paul, Hebrews 6:18, if we examine the original text, the Apostle does not simply say "God cannot lie" but rather that "it is impossible for God to lie": ἐν οἷς ἀδύνατον Θεῷ ψεύσασθαι [in which it is impossible for God to lie]. It is important to note that these are not mere synonyms but rather distinct expressions. "God cannot lie" and "it is impossible for God to lie" differ, as one implies an inability or powerlessness in God, while the other does not. For if I further say (to make the matter even clearer) that God could lie or break His word, I must say that this would be weakness, since God would not be able to do everything. But rather, God can do all things and is omnipotent, and nothing can prevent Him from keeping His word. For He is also *immutabilis* [unchangeable], and therefore, He does not end or break His word and promise. Thus, it cannot at all be proven from Paul's words that the opposite is intended; in fact, his words overturn that notion entirely.

Secondly, when it is said that God cannot deny Himself or cannot die, the word "can" (*posse, potentia*) does not imply an active power (*potentia activa*) but a passive power (*potentia passiva*), and thus an impotence. It means, then, that God is incapable of being powerless, or of denying Himself, etc. Similarly, being able to die means not being able to preserve oneself in life; that is, not being free or mighty enough to protect and defend oneself from death and corruption.

However, because God's power and *potentia* are simply and absolutely opposed to passive power (*potentia passiva*) or impotence (*impotentia*), containing none of it whatsoever, the ability to die, to lie, and to sin would be an *impotentia*—that is, a passive power, and therefore a weakness or inability—and, indeed, a suffering. Therefore, such things are not included in God's power.

Thus, when one says that God cannot sin, cannot die, or cannot deny Himself, it does not mean that God cannot accomplish something due to lack of omnipotence, or that He is too weak, or that His omnipotence does not extend so far as to do such things. Rather, it simply indicates that these things do not pertain to omnipotence but are opposed to it as a form of weakness.

Hence, this manner of speaking has this meaning: *God cannot die*, meaning God is immortal; death cannot overtake Him. *God cannot sin*, meaning God is so powerful in His righteousness and so immovable that no sin can befall Him. *God cannot lie*, meaning God is so omnipotent and unmovable in His truth that no lie can be found in Him or in His works. *God cannot deny Himself*, meaning God is so strong and mighty that nothing could compel Him to deny Himself.

For, as is evident, lying, dying, and denying oneself are not effects of power but of weakness. After all, who would say that a person is so weak, so unable, that he must die easily and cannot sustain his life; or that he is so corrupt and so weakened that he cannot guard himself against sin? Likewise, no one would say that God, with all His omnipotence, could bring about or accomplish that He would die, that He would sin, or that He would deny Himself.

But rather, it is attributed to the great power and omnipotence of God that such a thing cannot happen in Him, as stated. However, this is entirely different when reason says that God, with His entire omnipotence, cannot bring about, arrange, or create that a body, and indeed His own body, should be in many places at once. For here we are not speaking of *potentia passiva* and *impotentia*, but rather of *potentia activa*, of the actual working power of God, and it is said that it cannot do something. And with this, we are not, as in the previous examples, referring to *impotentia* or *potentia passiva,* in relation to the omnipotence and power of God. Rather, this power is limited and determined in relation to certain effects and is thus made into a simple and particular omnipotence, such that it is denied and instead attributed to God as a finite power and might. Therefore, there is a significant difference between how the Calvinists speak and how the apostles and the Church Fathers speak.

As for the other matter, the question is not how they speak—for that is obvious—nor how they later embellish or refine their words. Rather, the question is whether their words, as they have framed them, do not limit God's omnipotence, and whether they do not define it as a kind of potency and power that includes impotence and weakness, thereby rendering it particular, finite, and circumscribed. Danaus'[*] words are clear, saying, *Non potest DEUS omnia facere.* (*God cannot do all things.*) *Non enim potest montem sine valle facere.* (*For He cannot make a mountain without a valley.*) Here you clearly hear that Danaus limits omnipotence with respect to positive effects, thereby attributing to it something it cannot do. And this statement is cunningly opposed and set in contrast to the argument of the angel Gabriel, for he says to the Virgin Mary: *Nothing is impossible with God.* Danaus, on the other hand, says: *Something is impossible for God,* for He cannot make a mountain without a valley.

Likewise, Beza says in *Creophagia,* page 1, that God cannot do everything, for He is not able to make three equal four. But what does "God cannot do everything" mean, other than that He cannot bring about something absurd, such as making three equal four, or that what has happened should not have happened, since this involves a contradiction and lies? Just

---

[*] [1] i.e., Lambert Daneau (c. 1530–c. 1590), a French Calvinist theologian.

as the phrases "God cannot lie" or "God cannot die" have been explained earlier, so must these also be understood, namely, *sine limitatione omnipotentiae divinae* ("without a limitation of divine omnipotence"), and they should be expressed in words that do not imply such a limitation, as follows: God does not make or arrange that three equal four, which is not the same as if Beza were to say, "God cannot do everything." For this [Beza's expression] means, "God is not so mighty that He can do everything." But the intended meaning of that phrase is: "God is not so weak and powerless that He would lie, die, etc." To this we may add those absurdities that would imply that He Himself causes or permits three to equal four or that such things would happen through Him. And Beza's further words, in Volume I, page 300, are clear: *There are certain things* (he says) *that God absolutely does not wish to change, nor can He change them.* Likewise, in his sermon on the Lord's Supper, page 82, he says: *God cannot do everything nor change everything, for He cannot make it so that someone who has died did not die, or that twice ten cannot be twenty.* Through such ways of speaking, indeed, a limitation would be made on God's *potentia activa* (active power) itself, and not on *impotentiae extra Deum positis* (incapacities outside of God). This should be considered much more clearly, since he says in Volume I, page 299: *The phrase "All things are possible for God" HAS AN EXCEPTION.* That is, the saying "All things are possible for God" must be understood not universally, but with certain conditions. But this is wrong and incorrect if the saying is rightly understood, namely, of *potentia activa,* excluding all impotence and passive power. For this reason, it was also used universally by the angel and thereby greatly strengthened and confirmed the Virgin Mary's faith. For thus is the angel's argument:

> For whom nothing is impossible can also make it so that you, Mary, become pregnant without the involvement of a man:

> Now nothing is impossible for God; therefore, He can also bring about and make it so that you, Mary, become pregnant without the involvement of a man.

If the Virgin Mary had possessed Beza's wisdom, she would have said, "I respond to the first premise *ad majorem*, that it is incompletely universal; for it cannot be understood and accepted without some exception and condition. Therefore, the minor premise of the second statement must also be understood with conditions. In that case, is it so that God can only do certain things, that He can create and accomplish certain things but not others? Therefore, the question between you and me would now be whether God can do what I, who have never known a man, could conceive?" Thus, without any doubt, the Virgin Mary would have argued from Beza's foundation.

But she does not do that; rather, because she was full of the Holy Spirit, she immediately understood that the words of the angel must be understood *de potentia activa Dei* (in terms of the active power of God), and thus without any exception. Therefore, she promptly answers with these words: "Behold, I am the Lord's servant; let it be to me as you have said." That is, "I now believe it, because you have said that God can do everything without exclusion, even though I have never known a man and never will." But Martyr makes it worse, and even more grievous, when he says in his *Dialogo* against Dr. Brenz on p. 6, 10: "God cannot, with all His power, bring it about that a human body is present in more than one place at the same time. This is among the things to which God's omnipotence does not extend." Likewise, Piscator* writes in Volume 1, p. 77: "*Omnipotentia Dei est RESTRINGENDA*. God's omnipotence must be somewhat restrained." Who does not understand here that this does not refer to God's omnipotence as it is considered absolute, but rather an omnipotence as opposed to *potentia activa*

* Johannes Piscator (1546–1625) was a German Reformed theologian.

(active power), *passiva* (passive power), and *impotentia* (powerlessness)? And that is what troubles us greatly, for in this way God's omnipotence is diminished. However, it cannot help the current writers to argue, as if Beza and others continually add *salva & incolumi Dei potestate* (without any detriment to the divine power), for we respectfully believe that this is not always the case. Secondly, even if it were to happen, it would amount to the same as saying: "You are a dishonorable man; you do nothing that is befitting an honorable man, yet your honor remains unblemished. You are a coarse, clumsy, and unlearned fool, yet your courtesy and erudition, etc., remain intact." If one were to present such an argument to a modern Calvinist writer, would he accept it and abide by it, and content himself with such a limitation? I find it hard to believe.

Thus, thirdly, we gladly concede that God does nothing contrary to His eternal truth and nature. But we do not agree that such *non posse* [inability] makes a limitation, exception, or condition in the *potentia activa Dei* [active power of God], thereby implying that "God cannot do everything," or "God lacks the ability to do this or that." And the question is whether it goes against God's truth for Him to make a body present in multiple places. This has not yet been proven, nor can it be proven. Therefore, even if we concede this, it does not immediately follow, as in the words of the Calvinists, that we deny God's omnipotence.

12. *From this entire discourse, I understand that a distinction is made between the* potentia activa *(active power) of God and the* impotentia *(inability) or* potentia passiva *(passive power), which do not exist in God. And therefore, some things belong to* potentia passiva, *and others to* impotentia. *These do not in any way limit the omnipotence of God. This also includes those things which involve a* contradictio in se *(contradiction in themselves) and are*

contrary to the nature and essence of a thing. It seems evident that this is precisely what the Calvinists wish to assert.

Yes, it is often presented as such, but the question remains whether it truly represents itself in that way. We cannot believe this, for the facts are contradictory, in that they soon imagine something that runs contrary to its own description and thus, according to the reasoning of divine power (*ratione potentiae divinae*), is entirely impossible. They draw their primary conclusion from this: Whether a natural body could simultaneously exist in many places. But the question is whether human understanding reaches so far as to perceive, conclude, and affirm such a thing with certainty.

Man must, however, make a distinction here between simple contradictions [*contradictoria* ἁπλῶς], that is, between such contradictions which are in *manifestis* [manifest] and *explicit terminis* [in clear terms] and consist therein: as *Homo, Non homo* [Man, Not man]; *Deus est, Deus non est* [God is, God is not]. And between contradictions arising from qualification [*contradictoria in adiecto*]. When something is not immediately stated and simultaneously affirmed, but rather when, upon something being posited, something is added and appended to it, which by *consequentiam* [consequence] negates or denies the same. As if I were to say: White Blackness, that is *contradictio in adjecto* [contradiction arising from qualification]. For if it is Blackness, it cannot also be white. For White and Black cannot simultaneously exist in one subject.

That simple [ἁπλῶς] contradiction, because it is a contradiction without any conditions, is rightly said to be something that cannot exist or happen even in relation to God [*respectu Dei*], and that is because one side (*altera pars*) has the nature of Non-Being (*Non-Entis rationem*) or is compared to Non-Being, which is nothing, and therefore cannot have an effect, such as *Non-Homo* [Non-Man], *Non-Deus* [Non-God], etc. Rather, it remains certain that He (God the Lord) can do all that is something and can be something. But what is nothing, just as it is nothing, so it also cannot become anything. Therefore, if one were to say, *Deum non posse contradictoria* [that God cannot do contradictions], this *non-posse* [non-power] would be improperly understood, and would mean as much as, "God is so powerful, God is so immutable, that from Him no falsehoods, etc., which are found in contradictions, can be done or spoken."

As for *contradictionem in adjecto* [contradictions arising from qualification], which do not exist outright, but are elicited *per consequentiam* [by consequence] through what is added to a term and are made into a contradiction in the mind, I do not unreasonably recall what I have often taught and impressed upon my hearers; namely, that because the matter is often very obscure, and we cannot clearly see how closely the qualification (*adjectum*) conflicts with the essence or with what was first posited, in such contradictions, *in respectu ad potentiam et sapientiam divinam* [with respect to divine power and wisdom], we must carefully restrain our tongues, hearts, minds, and understanding, not bursting forth prematurely, and not judging God's power and wisdom according to the rules of physics and the wisdom, science, and power known to us.

Therefore, in this matter, it is first and foremost necessary to separate and distinguish between *God's* power and *our* power, and between *God's* wisdom and *our* wisdom. Then it will certainly remain clear that God's power and wisdom can do and comprehend more than all our senses and understanding are able to grasp.

If one proceeds in this way, then the next point follows immediately: that in matters that are more obscure [*in rebus obscurioribus*], with respect to the essence, power, and wisdom of God, we will not easily be able to discern what constitutes a *contradictio in adjecto* [contradiction arising from qualification], because we cannot know the properties of the essence, power, and wisdom of God. Indeed, it is impossible for us to know them, because they are infinite and indeterminate [*infiniti et indeterminati*].

Can it not appear that it is a *contradictio in adjecto* [contradiction arising from qualification] when one says that God is a single, indivisible essence and yet consists of three Persons? The Arians and Photinians affirm this. And if we look only at Holy Scripture and human reason, we might judge no differently, because no imagination or human reason is so strong and capable as to comprehend how an absolutely simple essence can remain simple while at the same time containing and consisting of three Persons, who are so distinct from one another that one is not the other and cannot become the other; namely, the Father is not the Son, the Son is not the Father, and the Holy Spirit is neither the Father nor the Son. Yet we must believe that this is not a *contradictio in adjecto* [contradiction arising from qualification] and that it rests solely in the fact that the infinite essence of God is of a completely different nature than finite creatures, so that His essence and existence cannot be measured or fully understood based on the nature of creatures or human reason. Instead, we must rely solely on the wisdom of the Most High, who has revealed this to us in His Word.

Likewise, it would seem to be a *contradictio in adjecto* [contradiction arising from qualification] to human eyes when God said to Adam: "On the day you eat from the tree of the knowledge of good and evil, you shall surely die" (Gen. 2), and then later: "You shall not perish, but you shall live." No angel or other creature could conclude otherwise than that, once man had fallen, he would be eternally lost, die, and perish. However, God's wisdom found a means to demonstrate and prove that this was not, in fact, a *contradictio in adjecto* [contradiction arising from qualification]; namely, by the Son of God taking on human nature in the fullness of time, making atonement and payment for the entire human race.

In the same way, who would not say—especially when setting aside Scripture—that it is a *contradictio in adjecto* [contradiction arising from qualification] to say that Mary is a virgin and yet is pregnant, and further, is a mother who has borne a son? "I can calculate it," says Luther, "and count it on my fingers, that no woman or virgin (to speak according to nature and reason) can become pregnant by herself. And it would not only be foolish but also a dangerous example if a woman or virgin were to claim that she became pregnant by herself. But here we have a master above us—God in heaven—who testifies of this virgin that she became pregnant and became a mother without a man. He has reserved this to Himself, that He has more ways of creating human beings than just one."

Who would not say here that being pregnant and being a mother contradicts the definition of a virgin? Who would not say that eternal death and dying contradict the definition of eternal life? That the Trinity of persons contradicts an absolutely simple essence [*simplicissimam essentiam*]? Indeed, it appears just as certain to reason that the notion of a natural body existing simultaneously in multiple places involves a contradiction [*contradictionem involviren*]—and yet it does not. What is the point of making much of this here? If the Calvinists cannot present this reasoning clearly from Scripture, where the matter is much more challenging, how much less can they apply it in this case?

From this, the Christian reader can easily see what a significant difference there is when we Lutherans say that contradiction [*contradictio*] does not pertain to divine omnipotence [*omnipotentiae divinae*] and when the Calvinists say it. Likewise, it is clear that we hold a very different view of contradiction in an adjunctive sense [*contradiction in adjecto*] with respect to divine power [*respectu ad potentiam divinam*] compared to the opposing position.

13. How many persons are there in the one indivisible divine essence?

Three: God the Father, God the Son, God the Holy Spirit.

14. Why must one acknowledge and invoke only three persons, no more and no less, in the Godhead?

Because God the Lord has revealed Himself in this way in the Baptism of Christ and in the institution of our Holy Baptism and other testimonies (Matthew 3, 24; Psalm 2, 33).

15. How is the Father described from the Divine Word?

God the Father is the first Person in the Godhead, who from eternity has begotten His only-begotten Son as His image, and who, together with the Son and the Holy Spirit, has created all things out of nothing and still sustains them.

16. What is meant by "God the Son"?

The Son is the second Person in the Godhead, begotten by the Father from eternity, and is the essential and perfect image [*Ebenbildt*] of the eternal Father. This Son subsequently became our Advocate and Mediator between God and fallen mankind. He took upon Himself human nature from the Virgin Mary and was born as a sacrifice for us and the sins of the whole world. For His sake alone, forgiveness of sins, righteousness, and eternal life are granted to us by the eternal Father.

17. What is meant by "God the Holy Spirit"?

The Holy Spirit is the third Person in the Godhead, who proceeds eternally from the Father and the Son and is sent to govern the holy ministry in the Church of God, and through the holy Gospel, He regenerates and sanctifies the hearts of the faithful.

18. How is it proven that the Holy Christ is God?

Romans 9: "Christ is God over all, blessed forever." 1 John 5 states that He is true God. Jeremiah 23: "They will worship Him as Jehovah our Righteousness." John 1: "My Lord, my God." John 1: "And the Word was God."

19. Why is God the Son called the Word of the Father?

Firstly, because He is the image of God, His Heavenly Father, in whom the wisdom, goodness, and essence of the Father shine perfectly.

Secondly, because He was the first to proclaim and announce the promise of the Holy Gospel to mankind, bringing it forth from the bosom of His Heavenly Father, and often repeating it in conversation with the Holy Father. Through this Gospel, He also works and brings about true knowledge of the Heavenly Father, new comfort, and eternal life through the Word.

20. Can it also be proven that the Holy Spirit is God?

Yes, very much so: In Matthew 28, Christ commands that Baptism also be performed in the name of the Holy Spirit. Since Holy Baptism is a covenant with God, and as we are baptized not only in the name of the Father and the Son but also in the name of the Holy Spirit, it must necessarily follow that the Holy Spirit, along with the Father and the Son, shares the same divinity, power, majesty, and glory. Furthermore, in many places in Holy Scripture, the name of God is given to Him, such as in 1 Corinthians 12:6; 2 Corinthians 3; Acts 5; Isaiah 6. Lastly, divine works are also attributed to Him in Scripture, such as creation, regeneration, giving life, omniscience, omnipresence, etc. Job 33: "The Spirit of God has made me"; Job 26: "The Spirit of God adorned the heavens"; Psalm 33.

21. So that we may return to the other Person in the Godhead, I understand from the description and from the second article of the Christian faith that He is true God and man in an inseparable Person, and thus in such a Person there are two natures: the divine and the human. If we are then further asked among ourselves and by those called Zwinglians whether the divine nature also communicates its attributes—namely omnipotence, omniscience, and the like—to the human nature, what is to be said?

Yes, for St. Paul says in Colossians 2 that "in Christ dwells all the fullness of the Godhead bodily." "All the fullness of the Godhead" means all divine majesty, power, and glory, which dwell in Christ, the Son of Mary. Therefore, He is also called "Christ," that is, "the Anointed One," because He is anointed without measure with the Holy Spirit and divine power.

22. Since the Zwinglians cannot believe this, I ask you to prove to me in particular that the Son of God has imparted His omnipotence to the assumed humanity.

I can sufficiently prove this with irrefutable testimonies from Holy Scripture. For we read in Daniel 7 that the Son of Man, who comes with the clouds of heaven, is given eternal dominion. Christ, however, is the Son of Man according to the flesh (Romans 1). And the Lord Himself testifies in Matthew 11 that all things have been given to Him by the Father. In John 13, the Holy Christ knows that the Father has given all things into His hands. This He also proclaims in His prayer in John 17. And He confirms and establishes this in Matthew 28: "All authority in heaven and on earth has been given to Me." But all authority in heaven and on earth is divine omnipotence. This has been given to Christ not according to His divinity—by which He has had it from eternity—but according to His humanity, in which He previously did not possess it. This interpretation is also explained by Theophylact and the unanimous consensus of all the Fathers.

Furthermore, we read in Ephesians 1 that God the Father raised Christ from the dead and seated Him at His right hand, which is nothing other than the omnipotence of God. Now, He raised Him according to His human nature, by which He had died, and thus also seated Him at His right hand in heaven according to the same nature.

23. Will there not, then, in this way, be two types of omnipotence in the Lord Christ—one specific to His divinity and another specific to His humanity?

No. Rather, there is only one singular omnipotence, which is common to both natures in Christ; namely, His divine and His human natures. Yet with the distinction that the divine nature possesses this omnipotence inherently, by its very nature and essence, while the human nature has received it from the Son of God.

24. Does not such teaching annihilate the humanity of Christ by transforming it into divinity?

No. For humanity remains a physical being and a creature, retaining its own human properties; namely, that it is in itself finite and possesses its own specific gifts. Of this, Luke 2 states that the Child Jesus grew in wisdom, etc. However, when one carefully considers the human nature in the personal union with the Son of God, God's Word teaches us (as has been proven) that the Son of God has imparted to His assumed humanity His divine omnipotence, majesty, and graciousness. Thus, humanity now possesses this majesty not as its own but as a gift from the Son of God.

25. How is it proven that God's Son has shared His omniscience with His assumed humanity?

Paul proves this in Colossians 2: "In Christ are hidden all the treasures of wisdom and knowledge." It is clearly evident that this is to be understood of the human nature, because divinity itself is divine wisdom. Thus, this wisdom lies hidden in humanity, in which the Jews regarded Him as a lowly and ignorant man. This was long foretold by Isaiah in chapter 11: "And there shall come forth a shoot from the stump of Jesse, and a branch from his roots shall bear fruit, and the Spirit of the Lord shall rest upon Him—the Spirit of wisdom and understanding, the Spirit of counsel and might, the Spirit of knowledge and the fear of the Lord. His kingdom will be in the fear of the Lord. He shall not judge by what His eyes see, nor decide disputes by what His ears hear. But with righteousness, He shall judge the poor and decide with equity for the meek of the earth." With these words, the prophet points to the human nature almost as if with fingers.

26. How do you prove that the Son of God has imparted to His assumed humanity the power to give life?

In John 6, Christ says: "Whoever eats My flesh and drinks My blood has eternal life, and I will raise him up on the last day. For My flesh is true food, and My blood is true drink." Here the LORD testifies that whoever eats His flesh and drinks His blood—namely, through true faith—has eternal life, etc. And He adds the reason: "For My flesh is true food, and My blood is true drink"; namely, for believers to eat and drink unto eternal life. 1 John 1: "The blood of Jesus Christ, God's Son, cleanses us from all sin." (Hebrews 9:14; 1 Peter 1:19; Revelation 1:6; Romans 3:25; Ephesians 1:7; Colossians 1:19 and 9.)

27. Is then the Lord Christ also with us here on Earth according to His human nature?

Yes, certainly. For aside from the testimony of others, the Lord Christ Himself teaches this. Matthew 18:20: "Where two or three are gathered in My name, I am in the midst of them." Also, "Behold, I am with you always, to the end of the world." We also read in Acts 23 that when the holy Apostle Paul was in great danger, the Lord Christ stood by him at night and said, "Take courage, Paul, for as you have testified about Me in Jerusalem, so you must also testify in Rome." Thus, we should have no doubt that if Christ wished to reveal Himself here on Earth, He could do so just as He did with Paul.

28. Does it then follow, according to the Christian faith, that since Christ has ascended into heaven, He can no longer be on Earth?

I answer and confess that, indeed, He was visibly taken up with His body, and a cloud took Him away from the disciples' sight, and thus He ascended into heaven. However, the idea that therefore He should no longer be on Earth with His body cannot be accepted. For the statement in Matthew 28:20 is against this, where He said, "Behold, I am with you always, even to the end of the world." Also, "Where two or three are gathered in my name, there I am in the midst of them." And St. Paul also testifies in Ephesians 4 that Christ ascended up into heaven, that He might fill all things, signifying that He did not ascend into heaven in such a way as to be only in heaven, but rather that, as the Son of God and as a man, He is present everywhere and, sitting at the right hand of God, fills all things—that is, He is present to all creatures. And this is not only affirmed in our Christian faith—that He ascended into heaven—but also that He has taken His seat at the right hand of God, meaning that He has become fully partaker of the omnipotence of God and now rules with God Almighty over all things in heaven and on Earth, a rule which is not absent but rather present everywhere.

29. What, then, is the right hand of God?

God has neither a right hand nor a left hand, as men do; therefore, the right hand of God is not a specific place in heaven, as some imagine. Rather, as previously stated, it is God's omnipotence, power, and majesty, which is present to all creatures. As God says in Isaiah 48: "He has spanned the heavens with His right hand" (that is, with His omnipotence).

30. It is also stated immediately thereafter in the Christian faith: "From thence He shall come." From this it nevertheless appears that He will return from the right hand of God as from a specific place. And thus, according to the Zwinglian view, is it correct that the right hand of God designates a certain place?

This is a futile evasion and cannot stand. For our Christian faith does not teach us, as the Zwinglians do, that the Lord Christ will return from the right hand of God as if it were a specific place. Rather, God's omnipotence fills heaven and earth; therefore, He can neither depart from nor be separated from the right hand of God, whether in heaven or on earth. Instead, He will visibly reveal and manifest Himself from heaven, just as He visibly ascended into heaven. This word "from thence" is explained in this manner by St. Paul in Philippians 3, where he says: "Our citizenship is in heaven, from whence also we wait for the Savior, Jesus Christ."

31. Can you further support your understanding of the right hand of God from God's Word?

Yes, indeed. Since the right hand of God is nothing other than the divine majesty, omnipotence, and glory, it is called the "Throne of Majesty" or the "Seat of Majesty" and "*dextra virtutis,*" the right hand of power. (Hebrews 8; Matthew 26). Also, "the right hand of Majesty" (Hebrews 1:3) is explained in this way, as well as in Psalm 8, referenced in Hebrews 2:6–8. It is further said that Christ sits at the right hand on the throne of God. Therefore, just as God's Majesty and Power cannot be confined to a specific place, so neither can, nor should, we understand references to His throne and right hand as referring to a specific place. Thus, in Holy Scripture, to sit at the right hand of God means to rule, govern, and exercise power and authority over all things. This is explained in Psalm 110 and in 1 Corinthians 15:25: "He must reign until He has put all His enemies under His feet." Hebrews 2:8: "You have put all things under His feet," meaning that everything has been subjected to Him, with nothing left that is not subject to Him. Hebrews 8:1: "We have such a High Priest, who sits at the right hand of the throne of the Majesty in heaven." Hebrews 12:2: And He is seated on the throne of God. Acts 2:32: "He is exalted by the right hand of God."

32. According to which nature has Christ been seated at the right hand of God?

Not according to the divine nature, which is itself the right hand or omnipotence of God, but according to the assumed human nature, which was once conceived in the virginal body of Mary and previously did not possess such omnipotence. For the Apostle Paul explains this article in this way in Ephesians 1: that God the Father raised Christ from the dead (He raised Him, however, according to the nature in which He had died, namely, the human nature) and seated Him at His right hand in heaven. And to help us understand this better, Paul says that He has placed Him above all principality, power, and everything that can be named in this world and in the world to come, indeed, He has put all things under His feet. By this, the Apostle indicates that Christ, in His humanity, has been set at the right hand of God in such a way that He now reigns with God the Lord over all creatures in heaven and on earth, and thus has all power and shares in Divine Majesty and authority.

On the Holy Gospel and the Promises of God, also Divine Providence.

33. It was previously stated that the Lord Christ first revealed the holy Gospel from the bosom of His heavenly Father. So now explain, what is the Gospel?

The Gospel is a promise concerning Christ. Or, it is a teaching that surpasses natural understanding, brought forth from the secret counsel of God through the Son, in which God the Lord, out of pure grace and mercy, for the sake of His beloved Son Christ, promises us freely the forgiveness of sins, righteousness, and the Holy Spirit to all those who truly repent and, through true faith, embrace and grasp the promised blessings.

34. What is the difference between the Law and the Gospel?

Three main differences are presented.

(1) The Law is, to some extent, known by nature (Romans 1, 2). But the Gospel is not known at all by nature; rather, it is revealed by the Son of God (John 1; Ephesians 3; Romans 16; Genesis 3).

(2) The Law promises righteousness and life, but with the condition that one keeps it perfectly (Romans 10). However, the Gospel promises the forgiveness of sins, righteousness, and eternal life freely, solely for the sake of the Lord Christ, and not because of obedience to the Law (Romans 3, 4, 10).

(3) The Law does not make anyone righteous; it does not redeem anyone from sins; it does not bring salvation. Rather, it only accuses us; it reveals and magnifies sin and condemns all people because of sin (Deuteronomy 17; Romans 3, 4, 5, 8; Galatians 3; 1 Corinthians 15). But the Gospel is the power of God to bring salvation to all who believe, and solely for Christ's sake, it grants believers the forgiveness of sins, righteousness, and eternal life (Romans 1, 3).

35. Are these promises of the Holy Gospel concerning Christ universal; that is, do they apply to all people?

Yes, certainly. For they are indeed offered to all people, whether they are believers or unbelievers, whether they are penitent or impenitent. However, only believers and the penitent partake of them, since only these apply and appropriate them to themselves through faith. The unbelievers and godless, however, are deprived of them and do not partake of them through their own fault, since through unbelief and impenitence they reject and cast them away from themselves.

36. If this is so, then I would also conclude that Christ died for all people, both believers and unbelievers, penitent and impenitent?

Although the Zwinglians may deny this, nevertheless it is certain that Christ died for all people. For John says in his first epistle, chapter 2: "My dear children, if we sin, we have an advocate with the Father—Jesus Christ, the righteous one. He is the atoning sacrifice for our sins, and not only for ours, but also for the sins of the whole world."

Here John says that Christ has become an atonement or satisfaction not only for our sins but also for the sins of the whole world—that is, for all people, believers and unbelievers, penitent and impenitent, excluding no one. For if St. John had meant that Christ was only for the believers and the penitent, he would have stopped at the words "for our sins" and would not have added "and also for the sins of the whole world."

37. Since Christ died for everyone, why then is not everyone saved?

The reason is quickly stated; namely, because not everyone believes in Him. For those who live in unbelief and godlessness and die in that state are condemned, as the Lord says in Mark 16: "Whoever does not believe will be condemned." Likewise, 1 Corinthians 6: "Neither the greedy, nor idolaters, nor adulterers, etc., will inherit the kingdom of God."

38. So then, has God the Lord predestined certain people—even the majority of humanity—to hell in His secret counsel from eternity, and has He also created them for that purpose, as the Calvinists teach?

No, God the Lord has neither predestined nor created anyone for damnation. For He has no secret counsel that contradicts His revealed will. Rather, what God presents to us in His holy Word—that is His counsel. Now God has, in Ezekiel 18:33, sworn an oath: "As surely as I live," says the Lord, "I have no pleasure in the death of the wicked, but that the wicked turn from his way and live." Here God testifies with an oath, "As surely as I live, as surely as He is God," that He does not desire that any wicked person remain in his sins and thus be condemned, but that all the godless should repent and be saved. How, then, could God have a secret, contrary counsel by which He would ordain or create the majority of the world for damnation? St. Paul also says in 1 Timothy 2: "God desires all people to be saved and to come to the knowledge of the truth."

39. If God wants all people to be saved, why does it not happen?

This question has already been answered. The fault is not with God, who offers His grace to all people in His Son Christ, but the fault lies with the godless themselves, who persistently disobey the Gospel. As the Lord says, "O Israel, you bring disaster upon yourself," etc. Likewise, St. Paul says in Romans 11 that the Jews have been broken off from the olive tree of the Christian Church because of their unbelief, but we remain standing through faith.

40. How do you know that you are chosen by God for eternal life?

I know this from the Holy Gospel of Christ, which teaches me that all who truly believe in Christ are chosen for eternal life. For thus Christ says in John 3: "For God so loved the world that He gave His only begotten Son, that whoever believes in Him shall not perish but have eternal life." Since I also believe in Christ—that He is in one person both God and man and has redeemed me through His suffering and death from all my sins and obtained for me eternal life—I know that I will not be lost but rather will be saved and inherit eternal blessedness.

41. Do you also know whether God will keep you in faith until the end?

Yes, I am completely certain of this. For God has promised it to me and to all believers: If we call upon Him for perseverance in faith, He will grant it to us. For the Lord Christ says in John 10, "No one will snatch My sheep out of My hand." Likewise, St. Paul says in Philippians 1, "I am confident of this, that He who began a good work in you will bring it to completion on the day of Jesus Christ." Here Paul testifies that God, who has begun the work of His knowledge in us, will also complete it. Likewise, in Romans 8, he says, "I am convinced that neither death nor life, neither angels nor rulers, nor powers, neither things present nor things to come, neither height nor depth, nor any other creature will be able to separate us from the love of God that is in Christ Jesus, our Lord." Paul also testifies that God loves us so dearly in His Son Christ that neither life nor death nor any creature can separate us from this love, unless we ourselves separate from Him through godlessness.

42. But I often find that I am weak in my faith.

The holy David also frequently laments this in his Psalms, yet he says in Psalm 55: "Cast your burden on the Lord; He will sustain you and will not allow the righteous to be moved forever." And the prophet Isaiah foretells in chapter 42 of our Lord Christ that "He will not break the bruised reed, nor will He quench the smoldering wick." From this, know that

God, in His love, does not reject such faith in us but saves us through it; for even weak faith saves, as St. Paul says in Romans 14: "God also accepts the weak."

43. Since we further believe and confess in our Christian faith a Holy Christian Church and a Communion of Saints, I also understand that what has been discussed so far, and what will also be discussed in the future, takes place in the Christian fellowship and Church. Would you please explain further what the Christian Church is?

The Church of Christ is an assembly of people in which the Holy Gospel is taught and preached, and the Holy Sacraments are rightly administered. In this assembly, there will always be some who truly believe, are governed by the Holy Spirit, and are co-heirs of eternal life and salvation.

44. What are the marks of a true Church?

The marks of a true Church are three: two primary and one secondary.

45. Is not the Holy Christian Church a body?

Indeed, it is. But it is not a natural or mathematical body; rather, it is a spiritual body (1 Cor. 10:17; Eph. 4:4).

46. If it is a body, then will it also have a head?

That is also true. But just as the Church is a body, indeed a glorious and beautiful body without blemish or multiple heads, it has only one head, which is Christ. Thus, Christ is the head of His Church, just as a man is the head of his wife, and in turn, the man is the head of his wife, just as Christ is the head of the congregation (Eph. 5:23; Eph. 1:22–23; Eph. 4:15; Col. 4:10; Col. 1:10).

47. Is there further thought given to the forgiveness of sins? Where are sins forgiven?

Only in the Church of Christ, for outside the Church there is no salvation. However, further discussion on this will occur below in the fifth part.

48. Do we also believe in a resurrection of the dead?

Yes, we believe in it blessedly, and therein lies our greatest comfort. For what could be more miserable in the world than a Christian if we did not have hope in the resurrection and victory over death? And this resurrection is already confirmed in the Old and New Testaments by examples. In the Old Testament: 1. The son of the widow at Zarephath, who was raised from the dead by the prophet Elijah (1 Kings 17:22). 2. The son of the Shunammite woman, who was brought to life by Elisha (2 Kings 4:32). 3. The man who touched Elisha's bones and was revived (2 Kings 13:21).

In the New Testament: 1. The daughter of Jairus (Matthew 9:25). 2. The only son of the widow at Nain (Luke 7:15). 3. Lazarus of Bethany (John 11:43). 4. The Lord Christ Himself (Matthew 28:6), whose resurrection is the foundation and cause of our resurrection (1 Corinthians 15:16, 20). 5. The saints who rose with Christ (Matthew 27:52–53). 6. Tabitha, who was raised by Peter in Joppa (Acts 9:40).

49. When will the general resurrection take place?

On the Last Day, at the final coming of the Lord.

50. What is the general resurrection?

The general resurrection is when, on the Last Day, all that is hidden will be revealed, and all the dead—both wicked and righteous—will rise. Their bodies, long decayed in the graves and turned to ash and dust, will be restored through Christ, who will come with thousands of angels, with great sound and thunder, in the voice of an archangel and the trumpet of God, appearing visibly in the clouds, just as He ascended into heaven. The bodies will be reunited with their souls, having cast off mortality completely, and will thus fully enter into life. Those who have not died will be changed in an instant so that, after death has been conquered, all people will be made immortal. They will stand before the judgment seat of God and receive eternal life—some in everlasting joy, others in everlasting torment—according to how they lived in this world and whether they believed in Christ or did not believe.

51. *Will a judgment also be held at this resurrection?*

Yes, indeed. For it is written in John 5:28, "The hour is coming when all who are in the graves will hear His voice and will come forth—those who have done good to the resurrection of life, but those who have done evil to the resurrection of judgment." Romans 2:5 also says, "But because of your stubbornness and unrepentant heart, you are storing up wrath for yourself on the day of wrath and revelation of the righteous judgment of God, who will render to each person according to his deeds." Jude v. 15 says, "The Lord comes with many thousands of His holy ones to execute judgment upon all, and to punish all the godless for all their godless deeds that they have done in a godless way, and for all the harsh things which godless sinners have spoken against Him."

52. *Who will then hold this judgment and be the judge?*

It will be God's Son and the Son of Man, our Lord Jesus Christ, who was judged for us, condemned to death, crucified, died, and on the third day rose again from the dead.

53. *I thought this judgment would belong to all three Persons?*

Indeed, this judgment, as an external work, is common to all three Persons (thus it is said in Isaiah 33:22; John 8:50; and 1 Peter 2:23 that God the Father pronounces righteousness, and the Holy Spirit is called "a spirit who will judge" in Isaiah 4:4). Yet the visible judgment will be carried out solely by the Son, and the Father and the Holy Spirit will judge only through the Son, who will appear visibly in the form of His human nature. (John 5:22, 27; Acts 10:42; Acts 17:31; 2 Timothy 4:1).

54. Will Christ conduct this judgment only according to His divine nature?

No. Since, according to Scripture, the power to judge the entire earth is attributed to Christ not only according to His divine nature but also according to His human nature, because He is the Son of Man. (John 5:27).

55. What will be the final sentence and judgment in this trial?

The final judgment will be twofold: First, for the God-fearing, who will stand on the right and hear these words and sentence from Christ: "Come, you blessed of My Father, inherit the kingdom prepared for you from the beginning of the world" (Matthew 25:34). Then, for the godless, who will stand on the left and hear these words and final sentence from the Lord Christ: "Depart from Me, you cursed, into the eternal fire prepared for the devil and his angels" (Matthew 25:41).

56. Will the execution immediately follow this sentence?

Yes, immediately. For as soon as the final sentence is pronounced, the execution will follow without any exception, delay, or appeal; namely, the God-fearing will be placed into eternal life, glory, and splendor, while the godless will be cast into eternal punishment and banished into the abyss of hell, according to the saying in Matthew 25:46, which follows right after the final sentence: "The (unjust) will go into eternal punishment, but the righteous into eternal life."

57. What, then, is hell?

It is a dreadful and abhorrent place appointed for damned people and evil spirits. (Numbers 16:30, 33; Isaiah 30:33; Matthew 8:12; 25:41; 2 Thessalonians 1:9.)

58. But where will this place be?

No one can know this in this life (Job 38:17, 19). For just as the apostles did not receive this knowledge from the Lord Christ, they also did not reveal it to the Church. Therefore, we should not trouble ourselves about it, but rather focus on guarding ourselves against that place, so that we may never come to experience it. May the loving God graciously protect and preserve us all from it.

59. But what will the nature of the pain in Hell be like?

No one can truly know or describe it. Just as no one in this life can comprehend the blessedness of the righteous, likewise none of the unrighteous can fully understand the damnation in this life, nor can it be expressed with words. Nevertheless, Holy Scripture often accommodates itself to us and our understanding by depicting these punishments through various images, such as a worm that ceaselessly gnaws at the heart, or as flames of fire (Luke 16:24). But this is not to be understood as the kind of fire we know, but rather, as Damascenus teaches (Book 4, *On the Orthodox Faith,* Chapter 28), it is a fire known only to God. These images are frequently used together (Isaiah 66:24; Matthew 13:28; Matthew 9:44; Judith 16:21; Sirach 7:19). Christ has also spoken about certain aspects of this hellish torment in general terms, describing it as a place of weeping and gnashing of teeth (Matthew 8:12; 13:42; 22:13; 24:51; 25:30; and Luke 13:28).

60. Will this punishment and pain be the same for everyone?

This punishment will indeed be great and severe for all

the damned, yet it will not be the same for everyone. There will be different degrees of it, as can be seen from Christ's words (Matthew 10:11; 11:22–23; Luke 12:47). Even those who will suffer the lightest punishment in Hell will endure pain and anguish incomparable to any pain or suffering that humans experience in this life.

61. When, then, will this punishment come to an end?

It will have no end but will be eternal, as seen in Isaiah 66:24; Matthew 25:41; and Revelation 14:10. This describes an indescribably miserable state for those people. Therefore, every person should indeed take care to avoid such incomprehensible punishment.

62. What is Eternal Life?

Eternal life is the state of everlasting and indescribable glory and majesty, in which all the elect, freed from sin and all other weaknesses, are fully united with Christ, their Head, in unspeakable and perfect joy, completely separated from all burdens, pain, sorrow, sighing, weeping, and distress. Together with all the holy angels and the whole assembly of the blessed, they will see God the Lord face to face, and will perfectly, with all their hearts, with their whole souls and entire being, without any weakness, praise, honor, and glorify Him. This will be a joy such as no ear has heard, no eye has seen, and which has not entered into the heart of any human.

63. What will happen to this world in which we now live?

Just as this world had its beginning, so it will also have its end and will pass away on the great Day of the Lord.

64. Some are of the opinion that it will not pass away, but will only be purified and renewed?

Yes, indeed, there are some who insist strongly on this. But what use is much disputing and contradicting, when God's

Word is clear and full of testimony that this world—heaven and earth—will pass away? Psalm 102:26 says, "You have established the earth long ago, and the heavens are the work of Your hands. They will perish, but You will remain. They will all wear out like a garment; they will be changed like clothing when You transform them, but You remain the same, and Your years will have no end." Isaiah 51:6 says, "Lift up your eyes to the heavens, and look to the earth beneath. For the heavens will vanish like smoke, and the earth will wear out like a garment." And Luke 21:33 states, "Heaven and earth will pass away, but my words will never pass away."

The Third Part
On Prayer.

How the Lord Christ instructs us to pray.

Luke 11, verses 9–10:
"Ask, and it shall be given to you; seek, and you shall find; knock, and it shall be opened to you. For everyone who asks, receives; and he who seeks, finds; and to him who knocks, it shall be opened."

1. What is the prayer that Christ has commanded us to pray?

"Our Father, who art in heaven, hallowed be Thy name. Thy kingdom come. Thy will be done on earth as it is in heaven. Give us this day our daily bread. And forgive us our debts, as we forgive our debtors. And lead us not into temptation, but deliver us from evil. For Thine is the kingdom, the power, and the glory, forever and ever. Amen."

2. How is the Lord's Prayer divided?

Into three parts: the Exordium or Introduction, the Seven Petitions, and then the Epilogue or Conclusion.

3. What is the Introduction?

"Our Father, who art in heaven."

What is this?

Answer: God wants to draw us with this, so that we should believe He is our true Father, and we are His true children, so that we may approach Him confidently and with all assurance, as dear children ask their dear father.

4. *What are the Seven Petitions?*

The First Petition

Hallowed be Thy name.

What does this mean?

Answer: God's name is indeed holy in itself, but we pray in this petition that it may also be holy among us.

How does this happen?

Answer: It happens where the Word of God is taught clearly and purely, and we, as the children of God, also live holy lives according to it—may our dear Father in heaven help us in this. But whoever teaches and lives contrary to the Word of God profanes the name of God among us. Guard us against this, dear heavenly Father.

The Second Petition

Thy Kingdom come.

What does this mean?

Answer: God's Kingdom comes of itself without our prayer, but in this prayer we ask that it may also come to us.

How does this happen?

Answer: It happens when the Heavenly Father gives us His Holy Spirit, so that by His grace we believe His Holy Word and live a godly life here in time and there in eternity.

The Third Petition

Thy will be done on earth as it is in heaven.

What does this mean?

Answer: God's good and gracious will happens indeed without our prayer, but in this prayer we ask that it may also happen among us.

How does this happen?

Answer: It happens when God breaks and hinders every evil counsel and will that would prevent us from hallowing God's name and letting His kingdom come, such as the will of the devil, the world, and our flesh. Instead, He strengthens and keeps us steadfast in His Word and in faith until our end. This is His gracious, good will.

The Fourth Petition

Give us this day our daily bread.

What does this mean?

Answer: God indeed gives daily bread to all people, even to evil ones, without our prayer. But we pray in this petition that He would help us to recognize this and receive our daily bread with thanksgiving.

What is meant by daily bread?

Answer: Everything that pertains to the needs and nourishment of the body, such as food, drink, clothing, shoes, house, home, land, cattle, money, goods, a pious spouse, pious children, pious servants, faithful authorities, good government, favorable weather, peace, health, discipline, honor, good friends, faithful neighbors, and the like.

The Fifth Petition

And forgive us our trespasses, as we forgive those who trespass against us.

What does this mean?

Answer: We pray in this petition that our Father in heaven would not look upon our sins, nor deny this request on account of them, for we are not worthy to ask, nor have we earned it. Rather, we ask that He would give us all things by grace, for we sin much daily and deserve only punishment. In turn, we too will sincerely forgive those who sin against us.

The Sixth Petition

And lead us not into temptation.

What does this mean?

Answer: God indeed tempts no one; but we pray in this petition that God would keep and preserve us so that the devil, the world, and our flesh may not deceive us, nor lead us into unbelief, despair, and other great shame and vice. And even if we are attacked by them, that we may ultimately prevail and retain the victory.

The Seventh Petition

But deliver us from evil.

What does this mean?

Answer: In this prayer, we ask in summary that our Father in heaven would deliver us from all kinds of evil—affecting body and soul, property and honor—and finally, when our last hour comes, grant us a blessed end and graciously take us from this valley of sorrow to Himself in heaven. Amen.

What does "Amen" mean?

Answer: It means that I should be certain that these petitions are pleasing to our Father in heaven and are heard by Him, for He Himself has commanded us to pray in this way and has promised that He will hear us. "Amen, Amen" means "Yes, yes, it shall be so."

5. *What should encourage us to pray?*

Primarily three things:

First, that God has commanded us to call upon His name and pray to Him in all our needs (Psalm 50).

Second, that He has promised to hear our prayers with certainty.

Third, that in the Lord's Prayer itself, He shows us and makes known the needs for which we should pray.

6. *You previously stated that the Lord's Prayer is divided into three parts: I have indeed heard the first two—the Exordium or Introduction, and the Seven Petitions. But you did not include the Epilogue or Conclusion.*

The conclusion lies in the word *Amen*. For in this word, all seven petitions are again included with heartfelt sincerity and true trust, so that God may graciously hear everything that has been prayed for.

7. Why, then, do you omit the words that seem to be the conclusion of the Lord's Prayer: "For Thine is the kingdom, and the power, and the glory, forever"? Doesn't this mutilate the Lord's Prayer?*

Yes, dear Christian, some opponents would like to interpret it that way, suggesting that when Luther omitted these words in his Small Catechism, he mutilated Christ's prayer. But if that were the case, then the Evangelist Luke would also have to be accused of this, since he also omits it in chapter 11, verse 2. Luther, therefore, did not omit these words without reason. Rather, he omitted them because they are not found as such in Luke's account.

Additionally, these words are also omitted in several of the ancient Greek manuscripts of Matthew, and they are not expounded upon by the early Church Fathers, such as Cyprian, Augustine, and Chrysostom, even in the places where they interpret and explain this prayer specifically.

8. Why, then, do we retain them?

This is for two main reasons. First, because these words are consistent with the entirety of Holy Scripture and particularly align with King David's thanksgiving in 1 Chronicles 29:11: "Yours, O LORD, is the majesty and power, glory, victory, and thanks; for all that is in heaven and on earth is Yours; Yours is the kingdom, and You are exalted as head over all. In Your hand are power and might," etc.

Secondly, because these words provide an exceedingly great and useful encouragement for the heart in prayer, as a model to acknowledge with holy reverence, to believe, and to experience that what we ask—"Thine is the kingdom"—means that God can deliver and save us from the power of the devil and all his forces and oppression, and also grant us glory. It is as though our Redeemer were saying: "When You, dear Father, hear us, it serves to extend Your infinite glory and honor."

---

* As may be seen, Martini does include these words in this book.

Thirdly, because these words are indeed found in several copies of the Greek New Testament.

Fourth and lastly, because they are also found in the Syrian translation.

Luther is rightly excused [for removing them] for three reasons:

(1) He does not dismiss these words as unimportant but retains them in his German translation of Matthew.

(2) They are not a necessary part of this prayer; otherwise, Luke would not have omitted them.

(3) The early Church Fathers also exercised this freedom, omitting these words in their standard explanations.

In summary, it belongs to Christian freedom to either include or omit these words here.

9. Should one pray "Our Father" or "Father Our"?

It is equally acceptable to pray "Our Father" or "Father Our," as is customary in some churches. However, as Master Brentz also points out in his Catechism, it is better German to say "Our Father." But to argue over this, as some Zwinglians and other Reformed do concerning the words "Our Father," is merely empty word-quarreling.

10. We say, "Lead us not into temptation." So I hear it said that God leads some people into evil temptation of sins and eternal damnation?

No, this petition is not to be understood in that way, for God tempts no one to evil (James 1). Instead, we pray in this petition that God would not allow or permit us to be led by the devil, the world, or our own sinful flesh into distrust, unbelief, despair, and other great shame and vice. And even if we are attacked by these, that we may ultimately prevail and keep the victory, as Luther rightly teaches.

11. Should one say "Deliver us from evil" or "from the evil one"?

It is equally acceptable to pray either, depending on the custom of a particular church. The terms "evil" and "the evil one" have a similar meaning, as the Greek word can imply both. By "evil" or "the evil one," we understand everything that harms God's honor or endangers our body and soul. From these, we ask God to deliver us.

12. When you worship the Lord Christ, do you worship Him according to both natures, or only according to His divinity?

The Zwinglians, indeed, divide the Person of the Lord Christ and openly declare that it is a questionable form of idolatry if one considers His human nature in worship and directs honor and invocation to it. However, this contradicts the Word of the Lord. For we are to call upon the whole Christ, since He is our Mediator and Savior according to both natures—divine and human. We read frequently in Scripture that He is invoked as the Son of David, who is such according to the flesh (Romans 1). Thus, Isaiah had previously prophesied in chapter 11 that the Gentiles would worship the Root of Jesse. Likewise, the holy people who worshiped the Lord bent the knees of both body and soul before His holy humanity. The wise men from the East bowed down before the Child Jesus (Matthew 2). The ten lepers (Luke 17), and the blind man sitting by the road, prayed to Jesus of Nazareth and called Him the Son of David (Luke 18). He is called "of Nazareth" according to His human nature, in which He was born in Bethlehem and raised in Nazareth, just as we could worship any aspect of His person even more. Therefore, if you wish to worship the Lord Christ rightly, you must worship Him as He is—namely, God and man—that is, according to both natures.

13. The Zwinglians claim to prove their position from God's Word.

For they say, we read in Isaiah 42, "I am the LORD; that is My name, and I will not give My glory to another, nor My praise to idols." Likewise, in Jeremiah 17, "Cursed is the man who trusts in man and makes flesh his arm, and whose heart turns away from the LORD." And in the Revelation of John, the angel says, "See that you do not worship me, for I am your fellow servant and your brother."

Now, dear Christian reader, consider their quoted Scriptures carefully, and you will understand that it [that is, the Zwinglian argument] is pure deception. For, notably, when God the Lord speaks through the prophet Isaiah, He speaks in clear, unmistakable words about idols and false gods, saying that He will not give or share His glory with them. Therefore, if this passage were to be applied to the humanity of Christ, that humanity would also have to be considered a false god or idol. But this is false, wrong, and a terrible blasphemy, since the Man Christ is not a different god but the true, living God. Even though His humanity is indeed the other nature within the Person of Christ, it is not another or separate Person from the Son of God; it belongs solely to the Person of Christ, who is both God and man. Therefore, when the honor of invocation is given to the whole Christ, who is both God and Man, it is not given to any other but to the eternal, true, living God alone.

Furthermore, Jeremiah speaks of the rulers of this world, upon whom we should not rely nor place our trust. Therefore, this passage cannot be applied to the flesh of the Lord Christ. First, because the Lord is not a prince of this world. Second, because Christ the Man is not merely a mere human; He is a Man who is also God, and thus His flesh is the flesh of God, as it exists in the Person of the Son of God. Therefore, whoever trusts in this Man or in this flesh does not rely on an ordinary human or common flesh, but rather on a flesh that shares its very substance with God's own flesh.

Third, it is also a great diminishment of the Man Christ that, now in His state of glory and majesty, where the Father has given all things into His hands, He should still be called and remain our Mediator. For even while the Lord was in His state of humiliation, He said to His apostles, "You call Me Teacher and Lord, and rightly so, for that is what I am." Now, if the apostles did this while He was in His state of humility, it was considered right, good, and well-approved by the Lord Christ, one may reasonably ask the Calvinists from whom they have learned that now, in His exalted state of heavenly power and glory, where He has received a name above every name, to be called upon in this life and in the life to come, they should regard Him as only their Mediator and hero. A sincere believer should be able to defend this truth and not be led astray by many harsh and strained arguments against the pure truth.

14. Can you also prove that the humanity of Christ was worshiped in the early Church?

Indeed: Athanasius, one of the foremost Church teachers in the East, in *On the True Faith to the Emperor,* along with Cyril in *Against the Theses,* 8, states: "If anyone should say that Christ's flesh, being merely human flesh, should not be worshiped, and therefore should not be worshiped as the flesh of the Lord and God, let him be accursed by the holy Catholic Church."

And Ambrose, a prominent light of the Church in the West, speaks as follows: "The angels worship not only the divinity of Christ but also the footstool of His feet. By 'footstool' is understood the earth, and by 'earth,' the flesh of Christ, which we still worship today in the Sacraments, and which the apostles worshiped in the Lord Jesus."

This means that the angels worship not only the divinity of Christ but also the footstool of His feet. By 'footstool of His feet' is meant the earth, and by 'earth' is meant the flesh of Christ, which we still worship today in the sacraments, as the apostles also worshiped the Lord Christ.

And Chrysostom, in *Homily 5 on Hebrews 2,* says: *Reverà magnum est & admirabile supero plenum, carnem nostram susum sedere, & adorari ab Angelis & Archangelis, Cherubin & Seraphin.* That is, "It is truly great and wonderful, and one should be astonished that our flesh is seated above and worshiped by angels and archangels, cherubim and seraphim."

And Augustine, on Psalm 99, says: "The footstool is the earth, and Christ took earth from the earth, for the flesh is earth, and He took flesh from the flesh of Mary. And because He walked among us in the flesh, He also gave us His flesh to eat and to share in." But no one partakes of the flesh without first worshiping it. Therefore, a way has been established so that this footstool of the Lord may be worshiped, so that not only do we not sin by worshiping it, but we sin if we do not worship it.

Since it has always been the unanimous consensus of the entire apostolic Church that the whole Christ, in both natures, should be invoked and worshiped, and since the Zwinglians not only act against this consensus but also oppose it to the highest degree, it follows that they cannot direct their "Our Father" to God. For no one can say, "Abba, dear Father," except through His beloved Son, who is not only God but also Man.

But we have this clear comfort, granted by God's grace, that when we call upon God the Lord in His beloved Son, we have such an Advocate and Intercessor who is flesh of our flesh and, in all weaknesses (apart from sin), has become like us, so that He can truly sympathize with us and is willing to help us. Therefore, whoever does not wish to be deprived of this great comfort should guard against this trivial wisdom. For just as you cannot speak with a person by separating their body from their soul and directing your words only to the soul, so, too, you cannot pray to the divinity while separating the humanity. Rather, you must address and worship Him who is both God and Man at the same time.

15. Is it also appropriate, when calling upon God the Lord in prayer, to kneel, uncover one's head, lower one's eyes, cover one's face, fold one's hands, or adopt similar humble postures?

Yes, certainly. This is a fine, praiseworthy church discipline, and God desires it as well. For although He primarily looks upon the heart, He also wants outward signs to bear witness to the inward disposition. Therefore, St. Paul says in 1 Corinthians, "A man, when he prays or prophesies, and has something on his head, or does it with a covered head, dishonors his head." This was also practiced long before us by the holy patriarchs: Abraham fell on his face when he spoke with God; Moses and Aaron fell on their faces; David lay on the ground; Daniel, Judith, and even the Lord Christ Himself, when He prayed, fell on His face.

16. What do the Zwinglians think of this?

Most of them hold that it does not matter to the Lord whether I have a hat on my head or not when I pray, as long as my heart is rightly directed. But one should not believe the Zwinglians more than the Apostle Paul, who opposes them, rebukes them openly, and clearly says, "No": for the sake of the angels and because the Lord, when he prays, does not have anything on his head.

17. When you invoke or mention the name of Jesus, do you also uncover your head and bend your knees?

Yes, I do so with great devotion and reverence, as it is God's command. For, as the Apostle Paul says in Philippians 2, "At the name of Jesus, every knee should bow, in heaven and on earth and under the earth."

18. Do the Zwinglians not regard this at all?

The Zwinglians do not heed this command; they consider it a ridiculous matter. For their forefather Calvin writes: *Plus quam ridicula sunt Sorbonici Sophiæ, qui ex præsent loco colligunt, genu flectendum esse, quoties nomen Jesu pronunciatum est, una habet inculsam.* That is, "It seems utterly ridiculous to him that the Sorbonne scholars in Paris conclude from St. Paul's words that one should bend the knee whenever the name of Jesus is mentioned, as if it were a magical word with some special hidden power." This is Calvin's notable judgment, which his followers eagerly adopt. When they hear the name of a Calvinist lord, prominent doctor, or teacher mentioned, they stand firmly, hats off, treating that name as something worthy. But when they hear the name of Christ, they keep their hats on, considering Calvin's authority far greater than that of the holy Apostle Paul.

19. But isn't it easy for error and superstition to arise, especially if common people kneel and bow their knees every time the name "Jesus" is mentioned?

Such an error can indeed happen, and not only among common people; even a learned person may mishear or think that someone is speaking of Jesus Christ when, in fact, another person is being referred to. But this does not immediately lead to heresy or idolatry if someone believes they are hearing the name of the Lord Christ, even if Jesus Christ is not actually named. For they are not showing honor to the person actually mentioned but to the One they have in mind—that is, Christ. Thus, some use this as an excuse to justify the practice and claim freedom in it, which many freely adopt.

The Fourth Part
On the Sacrament of Holy Baptism.

John, chapter 3.
"Unless one is born of water and the Spirit, he cannot enter the kingdom of God."

On the Sacrament of Holy Baptism.

1. What is Holy Baptism?
Baptism is not just plain water, but rather such water that is contained within God's command, namely, as the Lord Christ says: "Baptize all nations." And it is united with God's Word, such that the minister of the Church speaks: "I baptize you in the name of God the Father, and of the Son, and of the Holy Spirit."

Doctor Luther teaches concerning Baptism as follows.

What is Baptism?
Answer: Baptism is not just plain water; rather, it is water contained within God's command and united with God's Word.

What, then, is this Word of God?
Answer: Where our LORD Jesus Christ says in the last chapter of Matthew: "Go into all the world and teach all nations, and baptize them in the name of the Father, and of the Son, and of the Holy Spirit."

Secondly.
What does Baptism give or benefit?
Answer: It works forgiveness of sins, delivers from death and the devil, and grants eternal salvation to all who believe this, as the words and promises of God declare.

What, then, are such words and promises of God?

Answer: Where our LORD Jesus Christ says in the last chapter of Mark: "Whoever believes and is baptized will be saved; but whoever does not believe will be condemned."

Thirdly.

How can water do such great things?

Answer: Water does not do it, of course, but rather the Word of God, which is with and in the water, and faith, which trusts this Word of God in the water. For without the Word of God, it is just plain water and not Baptism. But with the Word of God, it is a Baptism, that is, a gracious water of life and a washing of new birth in the Holy Spirit, as St. Paul says in Titus, chapter 3: "Through the washing of rebirth and renewal by the Holy Spirit, whom He poured out on us richly through Jesus Christ our Savior, so that we, being justified by His grace, might become heirs according to the hope of eternal life. This is most certainly true."

Fourthly.

What does such water baptism signify?

Answer: It signifies that the old Adam in us should be drowned by daily sorrow and repentance, and die with all sins and evil desires. And that, in turn, a new person should daily emerge and arise, who lives before God in righteousness and purity forever.

Where is this written?

Answer: Saint Paul says to the Romans in chapter 6: "We were buried with Christ through baptism into death, so that just as Christ was raised from the dead by the glory of the Father, we too might walk in newness of life."

2. So, I understand—does this mean that Baptism is not a mere water bath, as the Zwinglians would have it?

Certainly not. For an ordinary, outward water bath is where one washes and cleanses the body's impurity with water, as stated in 1 Peter 3. But in Holy Baptism, sins are washed away through the blood of Christ, so it is a Holy, Divine water bath. Therefore,

St. Paul in Ephesians 5 calls it a "washing with water through the Word," and in Titus 3, a "washing of rebirth and renewal by the Holy Spirit."

3. If Baptism is a washing of rebirth, then must it not also work forgiveness of sins?

Yes, indeed, as our dear Luther has taught in short yet beautiful words; namely, that Baptism works forgiveness of sins, delivers from death and the devil, and grants eternal salvation to all who believe it, as the words and promises of God declare.

4. If Baptism has such great effects, then must it not also be necessary for salvation?

Yes, it is indeed highly necessary for salvation, since grace is conferred through it. For unless one is born again of water and the Holy Spirit, he cannot enter the kingdom of God (John 3). As with Noah in the first instance, when the ark was being prepared, in which a few—that is, eight souls—were saved through water, which now also saves us in Baptism, which is prefigured by Jesus (1 Peter 3). And just as with our Lord Christ in Galatians 3, that we are clothed in Him, so too we are justified through Christ (Ephesians 5), in whom we are washed from all sins (Acts 2).

5. Is this so? Then the Zwinglian view must again be wrong, in that they claim that rebirth and renewal are only symbolized in Holy Baptism.

This is a false teaching, since rebirth is not merely symbolized there but also actually accomplished. For, as just stated, a person is born again through water and the Spirit, and our Lord Christ does not teach that rebirth is merely symbolized by water and the Spirit, but that it actually happens through water and the Spirit. Indeed, Paul himself asserts this, saying that God has sanctified His Church universally through the washing of water—not only symbolically—but that this washing is actually carried out by Christ.

6. But Beza and other Zwinglians write that it is pure idolatry to attribute such effects to Baptism.

This is blasphemy. For since God Himself has bound Himself to it, it is not idolatry. As God promised in Exodus 30, "Where I establish the remembrance of My name, I will come to you and bless you." Now, the merciful Lord has established the remembrance of His name for all in the water bath of Holy Baptism. How, then, could it be idolatry for me to believe that the Lord will come to me *through* the bath and *in* the bath, and that I can also expect His blessing in this bath and receive it according to His promise?

7. Are all children reborn in Holy Baptism?

Yes, for the Apostle Paul calls Baptism a "washing of rebirth," which children cannot hinder through hypocrisy or stubborn willfulness (as might happen with adults).

8. That seems incorrect: For aren't only those children reborn who have been appointed by God to eternal life?

We should not let ourselves be hindered by such thoughts against the promise of God. Rather, we should consider the revealed will of God, which shows that all who are baptized put on Christ in Holy Baptism (Galatians 3). Therefore, since God has made known His divine will—and of this will Christ Himself is a witness—when He speaks of the little children, saying, "It is not the will of your Father in heaven that any of these little ones should perish" (Matthew 18).

9. Why is it, then, that so many of those who are baptized do not attain salvation?

This is not the fault of Holy Baptism, nor does it follow that Christ's merit and their salvation were not offered and given to them by grace in Baptism. Rather, it is because they do not make use of the gifts offered through faith or later, by living a wicked and godless life, grieve the Holy Spirit, who then departs from them with His radiance. Thus, through their unbelief, they forfeit the heavenly gifts, making room instead for the evil spirit. As the Lord Christ teaches in Luke 11 and John 15, some are grafted into Him, the true vine, namely, through Baptism, yet later, because they do not remain in Him and bear no fruit, they are cast out and burned in the fire.

10. In extreme necessity, may private individuals or laypeople, including women, be permitted to perform Baptism?

The Zwinglians say "No"; we say "Yes." For necessity is bound by no law, and the order of the Sacraments is not meant to rule over them but to serve them. The Sacraments do not exist for the sake of order; rather, the order exists for the sake of the Sacraments. Thus, Baptism, which takes place in cases of necessity, if administered by a layperson or private individual, is no less effective than if it were performed in the usual, orderly manner. Furthermore, as it is written in Galatians 3, "In Christ Jesus there is neither male nor female." We also have an example in circumcision, which was administered by Moses' wife, even though she was a Gentile, and yet it was according to God's command. Why, then, should it not please God if, in extreme necessity, women baptize? We also read in 1 Maccabees, chapters 1 and 2, that women were martyred for circumcising their children. From this it can easily be inferred that among God's people, it made no difference whether a man or a woman performed circumcision. Since Baptism has now taken the place of circumcision, what should prevent a woman from being able to administer it in cases of necessity?

11. What do you say about exorcism, which is still practiced in the Lutheran churches?

Exorcism is retained in the Lutheran churches, not as an idolatrous superstition or "devil's remedy," as the Zwinglians claim and therefore completely reject. Rather, we retain it as a free, indifferent practice in which we renounce the devil and all his works. And we do this primarily for three reasons.

First, for the sake of the one being baptized, so that he may be reminded of sin and later, throughout his entire life, be assured that he has been delivered from the power of the devil and, from being a child of wrath, has become a child of grace in Baptism (may God preserve us to teach such a thing!). For, spiritually speaking, they were indeed held under his tyranny due to original sin before being renewed and reborn through the washing of regeneration, that is, Holy Baptism, as Scripture testifies in Ephesians 2 and 4; John 3; Luke 11; Titus 3; and Isaiah 49 and 52.

Second, exorcism is used for the sake of the Church. For the witnesses present bear witness to their faith through this solemn command of exorcism, recognizing that miserable human nature, in which the child is born, is under the tyranny of the devil, and that there is an opposing power in the spiritual washing through which one can be delivered from the devil's tyranny and be assured that they can defy the devil. For when the minister says, "I adjure you, unclean spirit, to depart from this servant of Christ," it is as though he were saying, with the Apostle in 1 Corinthians 15, "O death, where is your sting? O hell, where is your victory? For the sting of death is sin, and the power of sin is the law; but thanks be to God, who has given us the victory through our Lord Jesus Christ."

Third, exorcism is applied for the sake of the holy ministry. Through this practice, we are reminded of the great power that the Lord Christ has permitted and given to His servants. For although the power to perform miracles—including the power to cast out demons from those who were physically possessed—has ceased, nevertheless, to this day, all true preachers, through prayer and with the help of God's Word, can tear down and overthrow the spiritual strongholds that the devil has established among the children of wrath and in the hearts of people.

12. Did the early Church Fathers also recognize exorcism?

Yes, for this is mentioned by Nazianzus in his *Oration on the Holy Bath*; by Augustine in *On the Sacraments*, Book 1, Chapter 5; by Cyril in the preface to his *Catechetical Lectures*; by Cyprian in *Book 4, Epistle 7*; and by Ambrose in *On the Sacraments*, Book 1, Chapter 5. Augustine's opinion on this is also repeated in the third holy decree, Book 4, Chapter 64. Thus, this ceremony was not, as some falsely claim, later introduced through papal influence, but rather was practiced in the entire Catholic Church over 1,200 years ago.

13. I understand from the reasons you have presented that you consider all children, before Baptism, to be children of wrath and of God's disfa-

vor, which surely cannot be true of the children of devout Christians, of whom Scripture openly testifies that they are holy?

Indeed, even all Christian children—yes, even the children of the most devout—are by nature children of wrath and outside God's covenant before Baptism. In Baptism, they are washed from sins, reconciled with God, and received as heirs of the eternal kingdom. Scripture testifies clearly to this, as in John 3: "Unless one is born again of water and the Spirit, he cannot enter the kingdom of God." And in Titus 3, Paul says: "Holy Baptism is a washing and means of the Holy Spirit, through which we are reborn and thus become children of God." However, when children are called "holy" in Scripture, this is not to be understood as though they brought with them an inner holiness of heart and spirit from birth; rather, they are called holy because they are regarded as children born within the Church of God and to whom the door to the covenant and sonship of God is soon opened; namely, through this Sacrament of Initiation.

14. But if it is true that Baptism is necessary for salvation, and that even the children of Christians—even the most devout children—are considered children of wrath, what should we think of the Christian children who die in the womb?

The correct answer is that these children cannot be regarded as having disregarded or violated God's order, namely Baptism. Since Baptism is a washing of rebirth, it presupposes and requires a first birth, which is of the flesh. For to be "reborn" implies that one has already been born. Therefore, for children who have not yet been born, Baptism is not commanded, and it does not harm them if they are not baptized. Rather, God the Lord works through the devout prayers of faithful parents and, without any intermediary, renews these children to eternal life through the Holy Spirit, forgives them their sins for Christ's sake—who Himself became a Child in the womb—to show that He can and will sanctify and save even little children still in the womb, if they cannot come to the ordinary washing of rebirth.

Just as the little children in the Old Testament who died before the eighth day, before their circumcision, did not violate or sin against the law of circumcision, since that law was given only to those who reached the eighth day and, therefore, they were saved without circumcision, so it is likewise with those who either die in the womb or at birth.

15. What should be thought of the children who are born but are taken away by an unforeseen event and thus do not receive Baptism?

God-fearing parents should commend these children to God the Lord in their prayers and should not doubt, for their prayer and sighs will certainly be heard and accepted by the merciful God, according to the sure promise concerning the search for the truth: "Truly, truly, I say to you, whatever you ask the Father in My name, He will give it to you."

16. It is indeed true that God will hear us when we call upon Him in Christ's name. Yet we also read in 1 John 5 that such requests must be proper and made according to His divine will. Who knows, then, if it is also God's will that parents should make such requests?

Yes, truly, it is God's earnest will, as He has solemnly commanded and directed that parents should always commend and intercede for their children's salvation before God the Lord. And God the Lord also takes joy in showing His gracious will in this matter, which He has mercifully promised and revealed in all things: "I will be your God, and the God of your offspring, binding and keeping mercy to a thousand generations for all who love Him." This is why He also wills that the little children should be brought to Him (Mark 10). Now, because in these cases of necessity, this cannot be accomplished by the ordinary means—namely, the washing of rebirth—it is done through Christian prayer, which, if offered in faith, penetrates the clouds and reaches the Most Holy One and is heard.

The Lord Christ has also sufficiently declared His merciful and gracious will toward young children when He says, "It is not the will of your Father that even one of these little ones should perish." From this, all devout parents can surely conclude that God the Lord, in such cases of necessity, will surely hear their prayer and that the

little children, thus commended to Him in prayer, are certainly received and accepted as heirs of eternal life and salvation.

The Fifth Part
On the Holy Preaching Office and the Office of the Keys.

Matthew 18.

"Whatsoever you shall bind on earth shall be bound in heaven: and whatsoever you shall loose on earth shall be loosed in heaven."

Romans 1.

"The Gospel is the power of God, which brings salvation to all who believe, first to the Jews, and also to the Greeks."

1. *What is the Holy Preaching Office?*

The Holy Preaching Office is such an office which is ordained by God, to preach the Word of God, the Law and the Gospel of Christ, in a public assembly of the churches, and to rightly administer and distribute the holy and most worthy Sacraments, also to announce the forgiveness of sins, and to absolve and declare free those who repent, but to excommunicate the stubborn. Through this preaching office God the Lord truly works for the salvation of all who believe.

2. *So I hear well, is power then attributed to the Holy Ministry?*

Yes, truly a great power, which exists in the Office of the Keys, of which the Lord says, John 20: "Receive the Holy Spirit. Whose sins you forgive, they are forgiven them, whose sins you retain, they are retained." And again Matthew 18: "Whatever you bind on earth shall be bound in heaven, and whatever you loose on earth shall be loosed in heaven."

3. So I understand that God forgives sins through the preaching office?

Yes, certainly. For the effect of the holy preaching office is eternal salvation, which God, though He could do so without means, chooses to work through the ordained ministers of the Church. Therefore, He has established this preaching office and uses it as an instrument. Thus, the spoken word (*Verbum vocale*) is like a vehicle of the Holy Spirit, and it has pleased God to save through the "foolishness" of the preaching of the Gospel all who believe in it.

4. How will you prove this?

This is proven by the fact that Jesus says to His disciples in Matthew 18:18, "Truly I say to you, whatever you bind on earth will be bound in heaven, and whatever you loose on earth will be loosed in heaven."

And again in John 20:23, Jesus breathed on His disciples and said to them, "Receive the Holy Spirit. Whose sins you forgive, they are forgiven; and whose sins you retain, they are retained."

Here, dear Christian, you hear what power is given to the disciples of the Lord, which is not given to the disciples alone but to all preachers in the Church, and was passed down through the disciples. Therefore, we should know and believe that the called servants of Jesus Christ act under His divine command, and especially when they exclude the public and impenitent sinners from the Christian Church, and when they receive back and absolve those who confess their sins and ask for grace, that it may be as powerful and certain as if our Lord Jesus Christ Himself were acting with us.

5. Do the Zwinglians agree with us on this point?

No, they do not agree with us, for they deny the effective power and working of the holy preaching office.

For thus says Grynaeus* in his disputation held in Heidelberg, Thesis 6 that when inner workings [i.e., of salvation] are attributed to the preaching office, they are merely words of honor. His words are as follows: "On my part, however, I honor the external ministry, but in sacramental terms, I attribute the efficacy of the internal ministry to this statement of Paul, 2 Corinthians 2:6, and in other places." See Beza in the second part of his *Response to the Acts of the Colloquy*, page 218, where he writes: "He greatly deceives himself and does injustice to God the Lord, who believes that God has given either to men, through whose mouths He speaks, or to the external Word itself, or to the sacramental sign, even the smallest portion of His divine power to renew people and to preserve them in Christ for eternal life."

A devout Christian should be warned here to reject these Calvinist denials and firmly believe that the holy preaching office is not an empty word or sound, but a powerful means through which the Holy Spirit kindles the fire of faith in the listeners, which is why the Holy Spirit was poured out on the apostles in the form of fiery tongues on Pentecost.

6. I have heard in the description of the holy preaching office that the repentant will have their sins forgiven: Tell me, what is repentance?

True repentance is when one is honestly frightened by God's wrath over sin, and because of the sins, feels heartfelt remorse and sorrow, and through faith takes refuge in the mercy of God, which is promised for Christ's sake, and firmly believes that, for Christ's sake, the sins are truly forgiven. Furthermore, though faith, one ceases from sin and orders one's whole new life in such a way that it aligns with the will of God.

---

* Simon Grynaeus (1493–1541) was a prominent Swiss humanist, theologian, and reformer

7. What are the elements in which true repentance consists?

Two. [First,] true remorse and sorrow, through which we fear God's wrath and feel remorse that we have angered Him with our sins.

The second is faith, through which we believe that the wrath of God has been reconciled for Christ's sake, sins are forgiven, and that through Christ we have a gracious God.

From this immediately follows new obedience, when we, in true faith, obey God according to all His commandments, so that God may be pleased.

8. Can no one have forgiveness of sins and eternal life without faith in Christ?

Zwingli indeed asserts that certain pagans were saved through a special mercy, among whom he especially counts the great disobedient sorcerer and idolater Numa Pompilius*, who, as Augustine testifies, first introduced all idolatry and delusion. Does that not mean proceeding rashly and carelessly in God's Word? If not, then I do not know. For Holy Scripture shows us the way to salvation, which consists in faith in Christ Jesus. Genesis 15: "Abraham believed the Lord, and it was counted to him as righteousness." Mark 16: "Go into all the world and preach the Gospel to every creature. Whoever believes and is baptized will be saved." Acts 4: "We read that there is no salvation in any other, nor is there any other name under heaven given among men by which we must be saved, except the name of Jesus." And John 14, Christ testifies of Himself, saying, no one comes to the Father except through Him. (John 5:24; Acts 13:38; Romans 3:22, Ibid. 4:3.)

9. Some refer to Luther, who also did this, in that he says that the pagans, Abimelech, Nebuchadnezzar, Hiram, and others were

* The second king of Rome, Numa Pompilius (753–672 B.C.) established the office of *pontifex maximus,* and the cults of Mars, Jupiter, and Romulus.

saved by what seems to be a fortuitous mercy of God?

Although Luther does say this, and holds it as true, they were not saved without faith and the ordinary means, but were instructed and came to the knowledge of the truth through the laws of Abraham and the Prophet Daniel, and thus were saved through faith in the coming Messiah. But this cannot be proven of Zwingli's godless pagans. And long before, Luther responded in this way to the Zwinglians in his commentary on Genesis, chapter 47, volume 6, Latin edition, Wittenberg, p. 686. In this passage, he opposes the Zwinglians, writing, among other things: "I do not affirm this with Zwingli, that Numa Pompilius and the like were saved and made heirs of the Kingdom of Heaven, but that righteous good men and women from the line and family of Cain heard the word and doctrine of the Fathers and by that faith came into the fellowship of the heavenly kingdom with the Church of the Patriarchs." That is: "Therefore, I do not say with Zwingli that Cain's church or Numa Pompilius, or the like, were saved and came into the kingdom of heaven, but rather that certain good men and women from the lineage and descendants of Cain heard the word and the teaching of the Fathers, and through that same faith, came into the society and fellowship of the kingdom of heaven with the Church of the Patriarchs." And just before: "Therefore, it is a very pernicious error, which we cannot approve or support. And yet I hear Zwingli citing my commentary on Genesis, where I said that some from the generation of Cain were saved, and I still teach this, but I do not say that they were saved as Cainites or Egyptians, but as incorporated and joined to the pure Church." Therefore, these people should be asked to desist from their irresponsible claims when they cite the words of Luther, as the devil quotes the Psalter, without carefully reading the whole text. If they do, they will find that they have done Luther an injustice before God and all of Christendom by claiming that he, like Zwingli, praised the salvation of the pagans.

10. It has been said that the Lord God forgives sins through the holy preaching office, but if my sins are to be forgiven, must I first confess them?

Yes, of course, you must confess them. First of all, the confession of transgression is a principal part of the pain and remorse that we bear over sin, through which we acknowledge our sin before God, repent from the heart, and lament it. We also confess that through our sins we have deserved the wrath of God and eternal damnation, and we are deeply sorry that we have offended God. Therefore, we ask for the forgiveness of sins for Christ's sake.

11. What is confession in the Lutheran Churches?

Confession in our churches consists of two parts: First, that one confesses his sins generally to the confessor. Second, that one receives absolution and forgiveness from the confessor as from God Himself, and does not doubt it, but firmly believes that the priest's [*des Priesters*] absolution is God's absolution, and thus through it all sins are forgiven before God in heaven.

12. What do I hear: Do the Lutherans retain private confession in their churches, which is still a Papal institution?

Here we say a clear "No." For private confession, as practiced by the Papacy, was long ago abolished in our churches; namely, the type of confession where one *must* recount and confess all of their sins, and where a special merit was attached to this recounting. This contradicts the merit of the blood of Christ, which is eternally and solely sufficient for the sins of the whole world, as 1 John 2 states. For, as Psalm 12 says: Who can discern his errors, how often he fails?

13. So, in Lutheran private confession, are not all sins recounted?

Indeed, when we stand before God without mediation

and fear for our sins, we should pour out our heart completely and confess all our sins, even those we do not know or recognize, just as we do in the Lord's Prayer.

However, in our private confession, not all sins are recounted. Rather, the person acknowledges generally that he is a sinful man. If there is something specific that troubles his conscience, he should share it with the preacher, openly confess it, and thereby seek comfort and forgiveness of sins with sincerity.

14. For what reason is this special confession and private absolution so strictly upheld in the Lutheran churches?

Because of the great benefit that arises from it.

First, since the ministers of the Church must not knowingly admit anyone to the Lord's Table who is not instructed in the articles of Christian faith, they can question and instruct each person in confession according to the Catechism.

Second, it has great benefit for those who persist in gross sins, such as gluttony, drunkenness, fornication, and disobedience against the holy preaching office and lawful authority. These people can be admonished through this means with seriousness to true repentance, to continue in repentance and admonish them to guard themselves, so that they do not fall back into their former sins. Or, if necessary, to exclude them from communion until they improve, so that the holy things are not given to the dogs, nor the pearls cast before swine, Matthew 7.

Third, if a person in confession is troubled in their conscience and has a secret concern, they can reveal it in confession to the church minister and receive instruction and comfort from God's Word.

Fourth, since it often happens that people question whether the general absolution proclaimed from the pulpit applies to them individually, the individual is strengthened in their faith through private absolution, so that they also receive absolution from the Gospel, and the forgiveness of sins, appropriated through the merit of Christ. As the Lord Christ often spoke absolution to individuals, such as to the paralytic in Matthew 9, and to the sinful woman in Luke 7. Likewise, the Apostle Paul excommunicated the incestuous man in Corinth (who had taken his stepmother as a wife), and when he showed evidence of repentance, Paul absolved him, granting him the forgiveness of sins in the name of Christ, and reconciled him with the Christian Church in Corinth.

This also agrees with our Christian Augsburg Confession and its Apology, which clearly states in Article 11, considering the great benefit of confession and private absolution, that they should be maintained in the Church and not allowed to fall into disuse.

15. Write me a common confession, which can be used by both the young and the old?

Worthy and dear Lord, I ask, please hear my confession and speak to me the forgiveness of my sins according to God's will.

I, a poor and miserable sinner (or: poor and miserable sinner [feminine]), confess here before God and you, His servant, in His place, that I, alas, am a poor, miserable sinner. From my childhood until now, I have grievously and exceedingly sinned against God and my neighbor with all kinds of innumerable, actual sins. If God were to deal with me according to His strict and righteous justice, I would have to expect His wrath and punishment, both temporal and eternal. For this reason, I carry a heavy conscience, and I continually hear in the ears of my heart the voice of God's righteous Law calling out and saying, "Cursed is everyone who does not continue in all things written in this law to do them." Yet, in the midst of this fear of my conscience, I lift myself up again and lay my head in true faith upon my Savior and Redeemer, Jesus Christ, and I am certain and believe with assurance that He has fully atoned for all the sins of the world with His joyful resurrection and has reconciled me with His heavenly Father, so that He has won and brought back for me eternal life and salvation. In this true repentance and sorrow, and with firm trust and faith, I now come to you, as Christ's servant, and ask that you would further comfort me with God's Word and grant me the holy absolution that God has commanded you to speak to me, and upon that, I desire to strengthen my faith, and I prepare myself to go to the Lord's Table, and there, under the bread and wine, receive and enjoy the true body and the true blood of my Lord and Savior Jesus Christ. I also earnestly resolve to amend my life with the help and support of the Holy Spirit.

Questions pertaining to confession:

1. *Do you believe that you are a sinner?*
    Yes, I believe it; I am a sinner.

2. *How do you know this?*
    From the Ten Commandments; I have not kept them.

3. *Are you also sorry for your sins?*
    Yes, I am sorry that I have sinned against God.

4. *What have you deserved from God because of your sins?*
    His wrath and displeasure, temporal death, and eternal damnation.

5. *Do you also hope to be saved?*
    Yes, I hope so.

6. *What comforts you then?*

My dear Lord Jesus Christ.

7. *Who is Christ?*

The Son of God, true God and Man.

8. *How many Gods are there?*

Only one. But three Persons: Father, Son, and Holy Spirit.

9. *What has Jesus Christ done for you, that you place your trust in Him?*

He died for me and shed His blood for me on the cross, for the forgiveness of sins.

10. *Did the Father also die for you?*

No. For the Father is only God, and the Holy Spirit as well. But the Son is true God and true Man, who died for me on the cross and shed His blood for me.

11. *How do you know this?*

From the Holy Gospel and from the words of the Sacrament, where His body and blood are given to me as a pledge.

12. *What are the words [of the Sacrament]?*

Our Lord Jesus Christ, in the night, etc.

13. *So, do you believe that in the Sacrament there is the true body and blood of Christ?*

Yes, I believe it.

14. *What moves you to believe this?*

The Word of Christ: "Take, eat; this is My body. Drink from it, all of you; this is My blood."

15. What should we do when we eat His body and drink His blood, and receive the pledge?

Proclaim His death and the shedding of His blood, and remember, as He has taught us: "Do this, as often as you do it, in remembrance of Me."

16. Why should we remember and proclaim His death?

So that we may learn to believe that no creature could make satisfaction for our sins except Christ, who is true God and Man, and that we may learn to fear our sins and greatly value His suffering, and take comfort and joy in Him alone, and thus be saved through the same faith.

17. What moved Him to die for your sins and make satisfaction?

The great love for His Father, for me, and for other sinners, as it is written in John 14; Romans 6; Galatians 2; and Ephesians 5.

18. Finally, why do you want to go to the Sacrament?

So that I may learn to believe that Christ died for my sins out of great love, as has been said, and that I may learn from Him to love God and my neighbor.

19. What should urge and encourage a Christian to frequently receive the Sacrament of the Altar?

For the sake of God, it should be both the command and promise of the Lord Christ, and also one's own need, which presses upon him, and for which reason such a command, invitation, and promise is given.

20. But what should a person do if they do not feel such a need or do not feel hunger or thirst for the Sacrament?

No better advice can be given to them than to reflect inwardly, whether they still have flesh and blood, and to believe the Scriptures, what they say about this in Galatians 5 and Romans 7.

Secondly, they should look around and consider whether they are still in the world and remember that sin and need will not be lacking, as the Scriptures say in John 15:16 and 1 John 2:5.

Thirdly, they will surely also have the devil around them, who, with lies and murder, will not allow him peace, either inwardly or outwardly, day or night, as the Scripture calls him in John 8:16; 1 Peter 5; Ephesians 6; and 2 Timothy 2.

The Sixth Part On the Sacrament of the Body and Blood of Our Lord Jesus Christ.

1 Corinthians 11.

"Whoever eats this bread or drinks from the cup of the Lord unworthily is guilty of the body and blood of the Lord. Let a person examine themselves, and so let them eat of the bread and drink of the cup. For whoever eats and drinks unworthily eats and drinks judgment to themselves, not discerning the body of the Lord."

1. What is the Holy Supper?

The Holy Supper is a Sacrament of the New Testament, instituted by the Son of God, in which He has ordained that we eat His true body with the blessed bread and drink His true blood with the blessed wine. He assures us verbally, according to the words of this Testament, that this takes place in a supernatural manner; and all of this is for the purpose that everyone who worthily partakes of this Sacrament may, through it—as through a heavenly seal of the evangelical record of God's grace and the forgiveness of sins, which He has given for us with His body and obtained for us with His blood—be specifically and particularly assured. Thus, with this food, we may be confirmed in faith in new obedience, remain in the Lord Christ, and He in us, so that we may live eternally.

Luther, in his Small Catechism, writes and teaches about this as follows:

What is the Sacrament of the Altar?

Answer: It is the true body and blood of our Lord Jesus Christ, given for Christians to eat and to drink under the bread and wine, instituted by Christ Himself.

Where is this written?

Answer: The holy Evangelists Matthew, Mark, Luke, and St. Paul write as follows: Our Lord Jesus Christ, on the night when He was betrayed, took the bread, gave thanks, broke it, and gave it to His disciples, saying, "Take and eat; this is My body, which is given for you. Do this in remembrance of Me."

Likewise, after supper, He also took the cup, gave thanks, and gave it to them, saying, "Take and drink, all of you, from this; this cup is the new testament in My blood, which is shed for you for the forgiveness of sins. Do this, as often as you drink it, in remembrance of Me."

What benefit does such eating and drinking have?

Answer: These words show us: "given and shed for you for the forgiveness of sins," namely, that in the Sacrament, forgiveness of sins, life and salvation are given to us through these words. For where there is forgiveness of sins, there is also life and salvation.

How can bodily eating and drinking do such great things?

Answer: Eating and drinking certainly do not do it, but rather the words that stand here: "given and shed for you for the forgiveness of sins." These words are, along with the bodily eating and drinking, the main thing in the Sacrament. And whoever believes these words has what they say and declare, namely, forgiveness of sins.

Who receives this Sacrament worthily?

Answer: Fasting and physical preparation are indeed fine external disciplines, but the one who is truly worthy and well-prepared is the one who has faith in these words: "given and shed for you for the forgiveness of sins." But whoever does not believe these words or doubts them is unworthy and unprepared, for the words "for you" require a believing heart.

Thus far Luther.

2. How, then, are they used in an adversarial way? For if this eating takes place orally, it does not merely concern an external matter here.

There is nothing adversarial in this. For when we say "orally," we are not speaking about *de modo sumptionis*, the manner of reception, as it is rightly understood and that the blood of the Lord is drunk. Rather, it should be understood solely *sacramentaliter* (sacramentally) that through the means of the bread and wine, we receive with the mouth the body and blood of the Lord *sacramentaliter*, not naturally, in a mysterious way that no one knows or understands.

3. How do you prove this?

With the words of the institution. For when the Lord Christ celebrated His holy Supper, He gave the bread to the disciples and said, "Take, eat; this is My body, which is given for you." Likewise, He gave them the wine to drink and said, "Drink of it, all of you; this is My blood of the new testament, which is shed for you for the forgiveness of sins." With these words, the Lord indicates that He offers to His disciples, and to all who receive His holy Supper, not only bread and wine but also, along with them, His body and blood. From this, we draw an irrefutable conclusion: What is clearly and unambiguously declared by the Lord Christ in testamentary form, with no change in the wording, as recorded diligently and consistently by three Evangelists and the Apostle Paul, as truthful witnesses and notaries, without any alteration of words or circumstances—this should be understood simply as it is said and written; namely, according to the common way of speaking, without any embellishment or veiling of the words.

Now, the words of the Holy Supper have indeed been spoken by the Lord Christ in a testamentary manner, clearly, without any ambiguity and without any change in wording, and have been diligently recorded unanimously by the three Evangelists and the Apostle Paul as truthful witnesses and notaries, without any alteration of the words or surrounding circumstances. Therefore, the words of the Supper must be understood simply as they are spoken and written; namely, according to the common manner of speaking, without any embellishment or concealment.

If this is indeed the case, then we will proceed further to affirm that we truly receive, eat, and drink with the mouth the true body and true blood of our Lord Christ, even though we cannot understand the manner in which it occurs.

The Calvinists may attempt to crack this nut if they wish. But if they want to attempt it, they must remain within the limits and dispute from their own standpoint, not from something that is spoken in Scripture about nests or Pharaoh's dream. Rather, they must prove their case directly against me and dispute my argument from their own foundation, basing their discussion on what is actually said in Scripture about this Sacrament. They must not bring in the analogy of faith concerning the article on Christ's ascension. For just as they may accuse me and say, "You must explain the words of the Supper so that they do not conflict with the article on the ascension," so I can respond to them, "Yes, you must also explain the article on the ascension in such a way that it does not nullify the words of the Supper, which were already instituted before the ascension." Rather, the explanation of both articles must occur in such a way that the words of the Holy Supper retain their true and proper meaning, and that the article on the ascension also remains intact. This is easily and rightly achieved according to our explanation; namely, that the Lord Christ truly ascended into heaven with His flesh and blood, yet still, in a mysterious and incomprehensible way, He remains with us according to His promise: "Where two or three are gathered in My name, there I am in their midst," and again, "Behold, I am with you always, to the end of the world."

I ask both friends and foes to consider the matter rightly, and to distinguish between a clear proof (*Apodixis*) and mere probabilities. If that is done, I have no doubt that one will give honor to God and refrain from further disputing against the truth.

4. How did the Lord give His disciples His body to eat and His blood to drink, when the Lord was still alive, sitting there, and did not put Himself into the bread, nor pour His blood into the cup?

This is a blasphemous question, and I must admit that I wrote it with dread. Nevertheless, since it is often on the lips of common folk and even found among the writings of the Zwinglian authors, I could not ignore it. But the correct answer is this: I leave it to my Lord and Savior to take care of that; after all, He is the foundation and mouth of truth, in whom there has never been any deceit, and He is indeed an Almighty Lord. Therefore, I firmly believe, and allow myself to be led by faith, without needing to comprehend how this could happen. What He says is true—that the bread is His body, the wine His blood, given for us—and that we truly receive His true body and true blood. Though I cannot understand how it happens, the Lord, while sitting at the table, gave His disciples bread and said it was truly His body, and of the wine, He said it was truly His blood.

You, disciple of reason, do you think that God the Almighty Lord cannot make His holy Word come true except in a way that you understand? And would you then cast aside all the miracles of the holy divine Scriptures, since they are all far beyond reason and nature? Therefore, dear Christian, if you want to be a child of God and Christ, you must believe the voice of God, your Almighty Father, who says, "This is My body," and not, "This is mere bread," which you eat in the Sacrament. If you do this, then you please God; and as soon as you wonder in what way it might be possible, remember what the angel Gabriel answered to the Virgin Mary's similar question: "With God, nothing is impossible."

5. *But to eat with the mouth, to bite with the teeth, to swallow down the throat into the stomach, and to consume: I hope indeed that you would not speak of the body of the Lord in this way!*

This, once again, is a frightening and abominable objection from the heretical Zwinglians. But, my dear child, do not be misled. For although we do speak of the act of eating and drinking that occurs with the mouth, we certainly do not intend to endorse such a Capernaite objection; rather, we oppose it with heart and mouth. True eating or drinking must happen in a described manner. Since we are not dealing here with natural ingestion—eating and drinking with our mouths—we must explain in our writings and sermons that this eating is sacramental, supernatural, in a way that no human reason can grasp or understand. So why would one try to impose such a blasphemous notion of eating or drinking upon us?

First, we teach that this sacramental consumption has absolutely no similarity or likeness to natural eating, which otherwise occurs with the mouth. Instead, through the medium of bread and wine, we receive the body and blood of the Lord. Secondly, the words—found in all three Gospels and repeated by the Apostle Paul in 1 Corinthians 11—say, "Take, eat; this is My body. Take, drink; this is My blood," and further say that all ate and drank thereof. Since the words of the institution remain so firm and clear, we rightly adhere to them and reject with great seriousness all manner of human glosses, whatever names they may have. For the Lord's Word is much more certain to us, as He told His disciples to eat the bread in remembrance of Him, and He called this very bread, which He gave them to eat, His true body, and the wine He gave them to drink, His true blood, which would be shed on the cross.

For those who believe and teach, like Zwingli, Carlstadt, and other similar followers, that it is only a metaphorical body and blood, signifying merely the power of the Lord's body and blood, and whatever further glosses they apply, this shall be said: When they are asked why they do not simply and straightforwardly remain with the words of the Lord and understand them literally, they respond with reasoning such as, "A body cannot be in many places at once." These are old responses derived from reason.

Reason, you see, can do nothing else but always say—because it speaks from natural principles and foundations—that it cannot be that Christ's body is present in many places at once, nor that His blood could be drunk from the cup unless it was first poured into it. But if reason reflects further on this mystery of the words, "This is My body," it must consider whose word this is—whether it is Calvin's word or God's Son's. If it were Calvin's, I would gladly concede with all Zwinglians and admit that such words must either be falsely declared or must have another interpretation. And then they might try to determine, with all their cleverness, whether Zwingli or Carlstadt had previously foreseen or observed this in some dream law, or whether Beza could later rightly explain it. For it would always remain doubtful what exactly Calvin meant with such clumsy words and ambiguous statements.

But since this is not a mere heretic, nor a mere human being far below, such as Zwingli, Calvin, etc., but One who is so exalted that He is called and truly is the Son of God—the Creator of heaven and earth, who has created and made everything that lives and moves, and before whom neither Calvin nor Zwingli is worthy to be compared—shall He, who has subjected all nature to His will, not be able to do as He pleases and as He has promised? Even if Calvin, Zwingli, an angel from heaven, your reason, and all the evil spirits say otherwise, then, if you want to be a child of God, respond: "You lie! I believe my Almighty Lord much more, who has said: 'This is My body' and 'This is My blood.'" If you remain steadfast in this, you are secure. And if you are indeed deceived, then you are well deceived. But believe this: God will certainly uphold His word and will not deceive you.

6. *Even though your words greatly move and stir me, faith is still very weak because I cannot comprehend how the whole Man Christ—His head, body, hands, and feet—could be received, eaten, and drunk.*

Such coarse thoughts are once again raised by the radical Zwinglians, but they ought to be ashamed to present such questions before Christendom. Now listen, my dear Christian: Set aside such fantasies and remember, as has been often said, that although the Lord Christ is truly present in His Sacrament, feeding us there with His body and giving us to drink of His blood in His presence, nevertheless it happens sacramentally, supernaturally, because it is a mystery. Therefore, this eating and drinking occur in a mysterious manner. Let not such objections of reason trouble you in the least. For if Christ were present in this manner, with hands, feet, etc., or in a quantitative way—according to the manner and measure of the quantity of His body—and were eaten as reason suggests, it would no longer be sacramental or supernatural, but natural. Then His presence would be given naturally rather than sacramentally.

7. There cannot be a body without its dimensions: length, breadth, thickness, etc. Therefore, if you place Christ's body in the Supper, you must acknowledge that it is there modo quantitativo *(in a quantitative manner), with and through the quantity of His body?*

It is true, dear Christian, that no human being and no reason can see how the substance of a body can be eaten without quantity, or how its blood can be drunk, or how, without quantity and according to the manner of quantity, the properties of a body could be in one place. We know and have long studied that quantity is a *proprium quarti modi corporis* (a characteristic of a body in the fourth mode), such an attribute of a body without which a body cannot naturally be in one place. We also understand that it is impossible for a body, in its natural mode, to be given, eaten, or drunk *per modum quantitativum* (in a quantitative manner).

But because we believe that the Lord Christ is not so rigidly bound by nature but surpasses it, for He Himself established and created the order of natures through His almighty power, reason and all philosophy cannot bring me contradictions or impossibilities in this matter. Should He not be able to arrange that the body *per modum quantitativum* (through quantitative means) or spatially located in one place can alter that order, so that His body, which is personally united to the Most High God, can simultaneously be in many places where the Holy Sacrament is administered?

It is worth noting that while the *exhibitio quantitativa* (quantitative exhibition) is a property of the body, it is not the essence or substance of the body itself. Rather, as philosophers know, it is an *accidens* (an accidental property), and therefore, a body in the *predicamento substantiae* (category of substance) can well be considered apart from this quantitative exhibition. Even though it is true that this consideration cannot entirely separate the substance of the body from its properties or its quantitative exhibition in understanding, it remains that reason must admit that the substance of the body and its property, namely the spatial exhibition, can be distinguished. Who among all philosophers and theologians would dare to say that God, who has combined these two things—namely, the essence or substance of a body and its quantitative exhibition—cannot make it so that the body can be eaten and drunk in a supernatural manner, rather than through the force of natural means?

I would still say, even alongside all philosophers and Calvinists, that such a thing could not naturally happen. However, to claim that God, who gave this power to nature, cannot, by His almighty power, accomplish such a thing is something I will not and cannot believe, no matter what Calvinist logic might argue. For such an assertion is contrary to His divine omnipotence.

8. Even though God the Lord is almighty, He cannot do what contradicts the description of a thing. Therefore, since it contradicts the description of a natural body that it could be simultaneously in many places, it cannot happen.

Although I do not wish to argue much here about what God can or cannot do—and it would be good if some Calvinists would hold back somewhat from such foolish thoughts—I must still ask them whether they know what the almighty power of God actually is. To this, they must answer either yes or no.

If they say yes, they must also admit what the incomprehensible essence of the Most High, Almighty, and incomprehensible God is, because the essence and omnipotence of God are inseparably one and implicitly the same. But since they must confess that they, neither with their reason nor with their understanding, can comprehend the infinite essence of God—because *finitum non est capax infiniti* (the finite cannot grasp the infinite)—their "yes" is meaningless. Rather, they must admit "no"; namely, that they do not actually know what the almighty power of God is.

If they do not know this, then they also cannot definitively say for all eternity that the omnipotence of God cannot establish or achieve something. For example, if I do not understand or know the power and authority of a great worldly potentate, how can I then confidently assert that he can or cannot undertake something? If I cannot do this, how much less can our reason, apart from the Word of God, say or know to say anything about the omnipotence of God—since it neither understands nor comprehends the greatness and power of God's omnipotence, nor can it comprehend or understand whether God cannot do this or that?

Therefore, it would be better if the Calvinists left such great mysteries and incomprehensible matters alone. Instead, let them simply believe, and they would not mislead so many people nor burden their consciences.

9. How could the Zwinglians not know what the omnipotence of God is, as it is described in God's Word?

Yes, dear Christian, the omnipotence of God is indeed described in Scripture, but only *ad captum nostrum*—that is, it is depicted for us and, to some extent, outlined for us *a posteriori*. However, such a depiction still falls far short and does not reach the eternal divine essence as it truly is and exists in itself.

Thus, when Moses desired to see the essence of God, he was given the reply that no living man can see or comprehend what His essence is. That is why God also responded to him, *Ero qui ero* ("I am who I am"), when Moses inquired further about God's great name. The Lord passed before Moses and allowed him to see Him from behind, thereby assuring him that if he wanted to see Him, he could comprehend Him only "from behind," that is, through His outward works.

This is also what Paul teaches: that we see divine matters in this world as if in a dim reflection. Since this is true, and our knowledge is partial, it would be well to refrain once again from this untimely curiosity and not concern ourselves so highly with what God's omnipotence can or cannot do.

Then it is further not validly asked whether these Zwinglians also know *quæ sit essentialis definitio corporis;* that is, what constitutes the essential definition of a natural body. In truth, it is evident that they do not know it, since they derive it from size, length, and thickness, and thus from the quantity of a natural body. If they do not know this, how can they claim that, through the words of God, the body and blood of the Lord Christ are dispensed in the Supper here on Earth, referring to the substance and essence of Christ's body?

Even though it is true that a natural body is a substance with size and dimensions that can be measured, etc., nevertheless, the term "size" or "dimension" is not the actual form or *differentia specifica* derived from its form. Rather, as mentioned above, it is merely a *proprium accidens* (a property or accident). Since you cannot assert or know what the form of a natural body is, and even less how a *proprium accidens* arises from its form or from the composition of matter and essential form, then no rational person—and no Calvinist, however deeply or highly learned he may be—can comprehend how far the omnipotence of God extends in this matter.

If they do not know this, then how, when the question arises about the divine power and virtue working in the Sacrament, can they draw conclusions about something incomprehensible from it? Reason, based on daily observation and experience, has long noted and learned that no natural power can accomplish this. However, to assert that a supernatural power also cannot accomplish it, they will never be able to say, for the reasons already mentioned.

10. Although I might concede to you that the Lord Christ can give His body here on Earth and His blood to be eaten and drunk, because it is the flesh and blood of the Almighty Son of God, it is still not proven that He wills to do so.

Proving this is not difficult, if only you would remove the thorns of your dangerous delusion from your eyes. We have the general promise of God's presence, which is particularly fulfilled in His Church, as stated in Exodus 20: "Where I cause My name to be remembered, there I will come to you." This promise was already visibly fulfilled for the Israelites when He was present among them as their guide and protector, manifesting His presence by day in a pillar of cloud and by night in a pillar of fire. This promise has always remained in effect and has not ceased even in the New Testament. We hear it reiterated in Matthew 18 with these words: "Where two or three are gathered in My name, there am I among them."

Here you hear the promise of the presence of the Son of God in every place where His name is remembered, including the Holy Supper. Specifically, it is promised that He will be present at the place on Earth where we hold and celebrate this Sacrament, feeding us with His body and giving us His blood to drink. Therefore, everyone can rely on the gracious will of the Lord; namely, that He will truly come to us here on Earth where He established the remembrance of His body and blood.

It is thus not necessary that I must ascend to heaven with my faith to partake of His body and blood there. Since this Lord is almighty and has willed to offer His body and blood to us here on Earth, revealing His will that He desires to do so, it follows that we must believe with certainty that here on Earth, through the bread and wine, we are fed and given to drink the true body and blood of our Lord Jesus Christ.

11. Even though I should be satisfied here, still, tell me whether the bread and wine are transformed into the body and blood of Christ?*

No, for the holy Apostle Paul, in 1 Corinthians 11, still refers to bread and wine in the Holy Supper, as he says: "As often as you eat this bread and drink from this cup, you proclaim the Lord's death until He comes," namely, on the Last Day. If it were no longer bread and wine, then St. Paul would not have referred to them as such.

12. Where are these words In, With, *and* Under *the bread found in Holy Scripture?*

Although they are not found in Scripture precisely as written, nevertheless they are included in the words: "This is My body, this is My blood." For since it has been shown that the bread and wine are not transformed into the body of Christ but remain bread and wine, and yet Christ affirms that He gives us His body to eat and His blood to drink alongside the bread and wine, it follows indisputably that we receive the body and blood of Christ *with* the bread and wine. The Apostle Paul also attests to this when he declares that the blessed bread is a *fellowship* or *participation*—as the Greek word κοινωνία literally means—in the body of Christ, and the blessed cup is a fellowship or participation in the blood of the Lord Christ.

13. *Do the words* In, With, *or* Under *the bread and wine signify a spatial inclusion of the body and blood of the Lord?*

By no means, as we have already denied this in the previous questions. Our belief is not at all that the body of Christ

* The issue in this question is the Papist notion of transubstantiation.

is enclosed in the bread or the blood of Christ in the wine, as straw or grain is in a sack, or as a core is within an apple. Rather, these words indicate only that I do not receive merely bread and wine, but together with them, I also receive the body and blood of Christ orally and truly.

14. What would you say in response to the claim that the Lutherans sing, Hidden in the bread alone, *which gives the impression that they believe a small body lies hidden within the bread?*

Such a notion has never occurred to the Lutherans. Rather, this is a freedom of expression employed in hymns and verses, which are occasionally used in such a way. Both Johann Hus, who originally composed this hymn, and Dr. Luther, who later revised it, intended nothing else by this than to teach or signify the true presence of Christ's body with the consecrated bread, which is limited to the very act of eating.

Moreover, the term *hidden* in this context does not mean *enclosed* or *wrapped up in the bread.* Instead, it means *mystical, invisible, incomprehensible to reason,* and *concealed.* Certain preachers ought to have considered this first before asking such mocking and blasphemous questions, such as whether one should believe that the bread is hidden in the body or that the body is hidden in the bread. Shame on you, devil!

15. What, then, does the Lord mean when He says the flesh profits nothing?

This cannot be understood as referring to the flesh of the Lord, since the Lord Himself previously stated: "Whoever eats My flesh and drinks My blood has eternal life." Rather, it refers to the gross, carnal thoughts of the Capernaitists and Calvinists. Just as in that time the Capernaitists disputed against the spiritual partaking of the Lord's body and blood, so too do the Zwinglians today dispute against the sacramental eating and drinking in the Holy Supper.

16. Would it not be better stated if one said that we receive the body and blood of Christ through faith, and the bread and wine with the mouth?

No, for although I readily confess that I ought to receive the Holy Supper with faith, and that without faith it is of no benefit to me, this manner of speaking—that one eats the body of Christ and drinks His blood through faith—properly pertains to the spiritual partaking of which John 6 speaks. In that context, only those who believe in Christ (which can also occur apart from the Holy Supper) spiritually eat the flesh of Christ and spiritually drink His blood. However, since in the Holy Supper even the unworthy receive the body and blood of Christ with the bread and wine, it follows that they also receive them without faith, and therefore only with the physical mouth. Yet this is to their judgment and condemnation, as St. Paul teaches in 1 Corinthians 11.

17. How do you prove that even the unworthy—that is, the impenitent and unbelieving—receive the body and blood of Christ?

I can sufficiently demonstrate this with irrefutable arguments. Firstly, when the Lord Christ speaks in the institution about the sacramental reception of the bread, which is His body, and the drinking of the wine, which is His blood, He makes no mention whatsoever of any distinction between the worthy and unworthy. Instead, He describes and assigns to all communicants a uniform sacramental participation. That this is true is as clear as day, because the Lord used one and the same form and manner of words for all. Not only John and the others, who received it worthily, but also Judas, into whom Satan had entered, was admitted to this Supper and partook of it.

The Zwinglians deny that Judas partook of the Supper, claiming that he left beforehand. That Judas was present at the institution of this Supper cannot be denied. For in Luke 22, after the words of the institution are recited, the Lord immediately adds: "But behold, the hand of him who betrays Me is with Me on the table," etc. Furthermore, Christ commands all to drink from the cup of the Supper, as Matthew testifies, and Mark explicitly states: "And they all drank from it."

Now, the question arises as to what it was that Christ commanded all His disciples—and, as Luke testifies, even His betrayer—to drink. This is immediately clarified by Christ Himself with these words: "Drink from it; this is My blood." And indeed, the words are connected thus in Matthew: "Drink from it, all of you; this is the blood of the new testament." The word "My" has particular emphasis here; thus, the Lord means to say: "I command you to drink from this cup, not in the sense in which I previously gave you the cup of the Passover lamb, namely, as a figure and sign of My blood, but as My very own blood of the new testament." Therefore, it is clear from these words that Judas, among all the others, also drank the Lord's blood (but to his judgment). The words of the institution are not altered when they are directed toward Judas.

All of this has been unanimously taught and written by all the ancient Church Fathers. And even if Judas had not been present, it would not change the essence of the matter, since they thereby admit that a sacramental reception and its efficacy rest in the words of the Lord's institution. These words were not established solely for the disciples present at that moment but for the entire Church, to be rightly observed and celebrated until the end of time. The Lord was certainly not unaware that the communion would be mixed, consisting of both good and evil participants, as He Himself foretold in Matthew 13. Thus, if any distinction were to be made in the sacramental participation or reception, the Lord would have made mention of it—even if, at that moment, all the disciples had been found worthy.

Is there more evidence for this?

The second proof we take from 1 Corinthians 11, where Paul states that the unworthy are guilty of the body and blood of the Lord. If they did not receive these, they would not be guilty of them. For, indeed, this conclusion follows from Paul's words. In this passage, the Apostle establishes the reason for becoming guilty of the body and blood of the Lord in the Holy Supper, by which the guilt is incurred and charged upon someone. However, this reason and guilt are tied to the unworthy eating and drinking.

Therefore, in this manner, as described and expressed by the Apostle, the godless become guilty of the body and blood of the Lord. Just as it can also be certainly concluded from Scripture that the soldiers of Pontius Pilate were made guilty of the body of the Lord Christ, the cause of their guilt, as the Scripture testifies, was their striking and crucifying of the body of the Lord Christ. Thus, the striking and crucifying are the cause of their guilt. From this, it is certain that even the godless partake of the body and blood in the Sacrament—but to their judgment and destruction.

19. Is it not shameful to the Lord Christ if one considers that His holy body is taken by the unworthy to their judgment?

Not at all. Since Christ is not only the Savior of the believing and righteous, but He is also the Judge of the unbelieving, as the Father has given all judgment into His hands (John 5). Authority over all flesh has been given to Him by the Father (John 17), and the power to execute judgment has been granted to Him because He is the Son of Man (John 5).

20. Is it one and the same body of which the spiritual eating is spoken in John 6 and which is referred to here in the Supper?

Indeed, certainly: for Christ does not have two different bodies. Therefore, it is evident that in both instances, the same flesh and the same body are being spoken of.

21. If it is one and the same body in John 6 and in the Holy Supper, does it then follow that all who receive the Lord's body in the Supper will be saved? How can it then be received to judgment?

Yes, if the eating and drinking in the Supper and in John 6 were of the same nature and manner, and if they were of the same body, then it would indeed follow that all who receive the Lord's body in the Supper would have eternal life. But because the manner of reception in both instances is distinct and different, and because the Lord in the Supper has sanctified and ordained a sacramental reception of His body and blood, which must occur under the forms of bread and wine, as a seal and confirmation of the other reception which happens through faith, it cannot be said of this sacramental reception what is said of the other eating, which happens through faith and has been in effect since the beginning of the world.

22. Perhaps the Lord, in John 6, spoke generally about the eating of His body and included this sacramental reception as well?

That this is not the case is clearly evident from the entire context of John 6. The Lord there neither referred to bread as His body nor wine as His blood, nor did He intend to establish or prophesy about the Supper. Instead, He spoke figuratively in response to the questioning and seeking of the Jews, who were looking for physical food and drink after having eaten from the five loaves. However, in the Holy Supper, He does not proceed in such a figurative or metaphorical manner when speaking of the eating and reception of His body. Instead, from His own intent, He instituted the reception of His body and blood, which is to take place through sacramental symbols. This confirms that the manner of this eating and drinking is not natural but supernatural and mysterious, as has often been taught above.

23. I have heard sufficiently so far that you primarily base your opinion on the words of the institution. Yet these words must be understood according to the nature of the Sacrament and the sacramental way of speaking.

I understand very well what you mean: the Zwinglians invent certain rules, which they dare to present to us as if they were confirmed by all the prophets and apostles. But they should know in response that we maintain that, although we willingly acknowledge and concede that there is something in which all Sacraments, in their kind, agree, nevertheless it is true that in each particular Sacrament, something unique is dealt with and ordered. Therefore, it is not permissible for us to fabricate our own rules in our minds that abolish the distinctions among the various Sacraments. For this reason, a devout Christian should oppose the Zwinglian fabricated rules by relying on each sacramental element, as it is founded and grounded in its own words, and judgment must be made accordingly. This rule will stand and must be upheld before the Highest Judge, the Lord Christ, who says that the one who does not accept His word will have a judge—the word that He has spoken will judge him on the Last Day. Likewise, His sheep will hear His voice and not the glosses and false rules of the Zwinglians.

24. Matthew 24 mentions the Lord referring to false prophets who say, "Here is Christ, there is Christ."

Here, a devout Christian should understand that the Lord is speaking at that place about false prophets who will bind the Lord to certain locations outside of a promise. However, where there is a promise, I may certainly seek Him, for wherever He has established a memorial of His name, there He comes to us and blesses us. Therefore, because He has established the memorial of His name in His Word and in His Sacraments, as said above, I do not become a false prophet when I seek Him where His holy Word is preached and the most holy Sacraments are administered, since God wills this and has commanded it most highly. That it is safer to remain simple and straightforward with the words is evident from the fact that the Zwinglians, in their glossing, are so inconsistent and bring forth nothing stable, but rather fall from one interpretation to another. For greater clarity, I will append some examples of their explanations.

(1) First, Carlstadt took the word "This" and interpreted it to mean that when Christ handed the bread to the disciples, He pointed to His body and said, "This is My [body]," or "There sits My body."

(2) Zwingli took the word "is" and taught that it means "signifies."

(3) Oecolampadius focused on the word "body" and taught that it refers to a figure, symbol, or representation of Christ's body.

(4) Calvin interpreted the words "body and blood" as referring to the power and efficacy of Christ's absent body.

(5) Beza introduced the concept of metonymy.

(6) The theologian from Polenzsdorf* brought in various figures of speech such as metaphor, synecdoche, and metonymy.

(7) Some seek a particular interpretation in the phrase "which is given for you," claiming it means "inasmuch as it is given for you," so that "This is My body" should be understood as "This is My body, insofar as it is given for you." This gloss is found in *Orthod. Const.*, fol. 14, and is also supported by Grynaeus in *Disput. Held. Thef. 19*. Keckermann** claims there is an improper meaning in the words of institution without a trope.

---

* The reference is obscure.

** Bartholomäus Keckermann (1572–1609) was a German Calvinist theologian.

These glosses are plentiful enough. If one doesn't appeal to you, you can turn to another. But my dear Christian, if you want to be certain, follow Luther's advice: Abandon the glosses and remain with the text and words. For, he says, "If I am to be deceived, I would rather be deceived by God (if that were possible) than by man. For if God deceives me, He will surely answer for it and restore me, but if men deceive me and I end up in hell, they cannot make restitution."

25. What do you say about the round wafers that the Lutherans use in administering the Holy Supper? Are they truly bread?

Yes, for they are made from flour and water, just like any other bread.

26. Nevertheless, it is claimed that the small wafers, as they are called, are not proper bread because they do not have the nourishing power of other common bread.

That this bread supposedly lacks the power to nourish, unlike other bread, has not been proven by any Zwinglian. And that the contrary is true is certain without doubt. For since they possess all the essential elements of natural bread and are even baked from proper white flour, how could it then be that they do not have the power to nourish and satisfy? Indeed, it has been observed that these wafers, when consumed in good quantity, truly possess the same nourishing and sustaining power as other bread.

27. Should the bread not be broken during the administration of the Lord's Supper?

It is an indifferent matter; one may break it or not. Therefore, if it has already been broken beforehand, there is no need to break it again during the Lord's Supper.

28. Did Christ not break it?

That is true, for it was not broken beforehand. Since the Lord had a large loaf of bread before Him, He did not wish to give them the entire loaf for them to bite off from, but instead, He broke it and gave each a portion. However, as our wafers are already broken bread, it is unnecessary to break them further; it suffices simply to distribute them. This distribution is also referred to in Scripture as the breaking of bread, as in Isaiah 58.

29. Nevertheless, Christ commanded it during the institution and said: "Do this." *Therefore, for God's command to be fulfilled, must the bread necessarily be broken?*

As for God's commands and institutions, we readily concede that all of them must and ought to be strictly and steadfastly observed. Therefore, if it can be proven that the words *"Do this"* must also be applied to the breaking of bread, as the Zwinglians claim, then the matter is clear, and we would have to yield to them.

30. They can certainly make this claim. For the Lord says we should do what He did in remembrance of Him. But what did He do?

1. He took the bread.

2. Gave thanks.

3. Broke it.

4. Gave it to His disciples.

5. Said: Take.

6. Eat, for this is My body.

Therefore, if we are to observe all these actions in the administration of the Lord's Supper, then it must necessarily follow that the breaking of bread must also be observed.

Here, it is important to note that "breaking bread" is taken in two ways in Holy Scripture, which we now briefly wish to indicate.

First, "breaking bread" refers to dividing a whole loaf into pieces. This was the manner in which the Lord Christ, according to Jewish custom and practice, not only broke bread at the Last Supper but also used this method in other instances, such as in His miracles (John 6).

Second, "breaking bread" simply means *distributing* bread, which can occur without physically breaking it into smaller pieces. This meaning is evident in passages such as Genesis 24 and Isaiah 58.

In the first sense mentioned, we consider it a matter of indifference (*adiaphoron*). While the bread used in the original institution required breaking for distribution, Christ broke it not out of necessity for the Sacrament itself but out of the practical necessity of distributing it.

Therefore, if the Zwinglians wish to interpret it in this manner and do not make it a matter of necessity, it could be a permissible approach, and we might find agreement in this matter.

However, concerning the second interpretation of "breaking bread," which, according to Scripture, signifies distribution, we consider this absolutely necessary and, in accordance with Christ's command (*Do this*), by no means to be neglected.

31. With what will you prove that the breaking of bread during the administration does not belong under the command (Do this) *but is instead a free matter of indifference* (adiaphoron)*?*

This can first be seen from the fact that neither the Lord Christ nor the apostles insisted upon this Calvinistic breaking of bread as a necessity. Furthermore, the opposing view cannot find a consistent example in the entire antiquity of the Church where the breaking of a whole loaf into pieces was made into such a Zwinglian necessity or used to establish a tyranny over consciences.

32. Doesn't the Lord Christ nevertheless speak of the entire action, saying, Do this?

To this, the proper answer is again given: This command applies to the parts of the action that the apostles carried out at that time; namely, that they should eat, drink, and remember the Lord in the process, as the holy Apostle Paul explicitly explains in 1 Corinthians 11, where he says: "As often as you eat this bread and drink this cup, you proclaim the Lord's death until He comes." Therefore, if the remembrance of the death of Christ consists in the Calvinistic breaking of bread, it would be false for the Apostle to say here that it consists only in eating and drinking—far from it.

Furthermore, if the command "Do this" is to be generally applied to everything Christ did, then the Zwinglians must henceforth use not leavened bread but unleavened bread, as Christ did; likewise, they must no longer celebrate the Supper in the morning but in the evening, not in the Church but in an inn, and not while standing but while sitting.

33. Even if this may seem to align with the truth, nonetheless it is a different matter regarding the circumstances of the time, the place, and the quality of the bread, compared to the breaking of the bread itself. For Christ did not say, Do this in the morning or evening, sitting or standing.

We gladly let that pass. However, if this is true, it must also be concluded from it that Christ did not say, "Break the bread into pieces." Therefore, Christ did not command it, and thus the opposing side strikes itself with its own sword.

34. Christ, however, broke the bread. Since Christ did so, must we not also do the same?

If this were to hold true, then it would likewise follow: Christ also used unleavened bread. Therefore, according to the Zwinglian view that we must do everything Christ did, it would follow that we also ought to use unleavened bread. If the Zwinglians wish to consider this without objection, they should acknowledge that, in their supposed freedom, despite Christ's command (*Do this*), they use leavened bread instead of unleavened bread, which Christ used. In this same freedom, we can, without violating Christ's command, refrain from breaking the bread into pieces and instead distribute it whole to the communicants.

Similarly, just as we are not bound by surrounding circumstances, such as the time, place, or location, we are also not bound to breaking a whole loaf or cake into pieces. Christ's command is fully fulfilled when one takes proper, natural bread and distributes it among the communicants. For this is the purpose of its institution—not that the bread should be broken into pieces, but that it should be distributed and, in its eating, serve as the participation or communion of the body of Christ.

35. *Nevertheless, it is argued that the breaking of bread during the Supper was commanded by Christ so that we might remember and be assured that His body was broken or put to death for us on the cross, so that we might not be broken, tormented, or tortured by the devil in hell for all eternity. Therefore, it is claimed that from such breaking of bread, great comfort can be drawn.*

Answer: That the suffering and death of the Lord Christ is our highest comfort, we gladly confess. However, the idea that this breaking or dividing of bread is meant to deliver or assure us of this comfort is a pure fabrication.

36. *How will you prove this?*

With irrefutable reasons. Firstly, it is impossible for the Zwinglians to prove that the breaking of bread was ever instituted by Christ for the purpose or reason of representing or signifying His sacrificed body through the breaking of bread.

Furthermore, although it is certain that there is a sacramental analogy between the blessed bread and the body of the Lord Christ, nevertheless it is far different from the analogy found in the Sacraments of the Old Testament. For the suffering and death of Christ in the New Testament is no longer prefigured, as it was previously in the Old Testament through the Mosaic sacrifices and the Paschal Lamb. In this case, the meaning would be even darker than that of the Jews, whose symbols were much clearer, brighter, and more apparent than ours.

No one can deny that the slaughtering and offering of the Levitical sacrifices, the shedding of their blood, and the raising of the bronze serpent in the wilderness were far clearer figures of Christ's suffering than the breaking of bread could ever be.

Thirdly, the Evangelist John has completely undermined this Zwinglian interpretation. By referring to the type of the Paschal Lamb, he shows that Christ's body was not to be broken in the manner suggested by Calvinistic bread-breaking. Thus, the Jews spared His body from being broken because it is written: "You shall not break any of its bones" (John 19:36).

37. Christ does indeed say, "Destroy this temple, and in three days I will raise it up," referring to the temple of His body. Likewise, Paul says in 1 Corinthians 11, "This is My body, which is broken for you."

Here is the correct response: Firstly, in both of these passages, there is absolutely no mention of the breaking of bread but rather of the breaking of Christ's body. Secondly, the word "broken" cannot be taken in its literal sense, as shown clearly by John 19, where it is expressly indicated that not a single bone of Christ's body was to be broken. Rather, the term is used metaphorically to signify the pains of His suffering and death, just as Scripture uses other metaphors when speaking of Christ's suffering, such as in Isaiah 53, Daniel 9, and elsewhere.

If the breaking of bread were necessary to convey such a meaning, then the Zwinglians would also be obligated to show a corresponding analogy in the cup that aligns symbolically with the shedding of Christ's blood. However, the wine is neither spilled nor poured out but simply drunk. Thus, it follows that Christ has abolished the clear prefigurations of His suffering and shedding of blood that were found in the Paschal Lamb and replaced them with a darker figure. This goes against the nature of the New Testament, which Scripture contrasts with the Old Testament as being like light compared to darkness (Romans 13).

38. *It is indeed claimed that the Pope is the author and originator of the practice of using wafers, and therefore they should rightly be rejected as an abomination.*

Although this is often said and written by the opposition, they have not yet been able to produce a single credible piece of evidence from Church history to substantiate this claim, even to this day. Therefore, we rightly consider it to be untrue. Furthermore, we can confidently point to the authority of Epiphanius in *Ancoratus,* where he makes mention of such round wafers.

39. *Conclusion: I do not agree that the Lutherans place the bread directly into the communicants' mouths instead of giving it into their hands, as the Lord gave the bread to His disciples.*

Answer: This is, once again, an entirely unnecessary and unfounded question. It is undeniable that such a matter belongs to the category of *adiaphora* (indifferent things) and free 'middle' matters. It neither adds to, nor detracts from, the substance and essence of the Holy Supper, whether the bread is placed into the communicants' mouths or given into their hands, as long as the eating of the bread is done with the mouth.

Conclusion.

Thus, we have diligently compiled this for the common people, primarily for their benefit, from the writings and teachings of the teachers of the universal Lutheran Church. We pray to Almighty God that He would protect and preserve His little flock, which He has now gathered and assembled through His Word in this deceptive world's twilight, from all manner of sectarianism and heresy. May He restrain and hinder the wicked Satan, who roams about like a roaring lion, for the sake of Christ, our Redeemer and Savior, who with the Father and the Holy Spirit lives and reigns, one true God, highly praised from eternity to eternity.

The End.

Follows a beautiful Christian and devout prayer for when one goes to the Lord's Supper:

Lord Jesus Christ, You eternal, almighty Son of God, our only Mediator, High Priest, and true Institutor of Your holy, most venerable Supper, who, out of heartfelt and unspeakable love and wonderful divine compassion, became man for our sake and gave Your holy body to death for us poor sinners, shedding Your holy rose-colored blood for the washing away of my sins and those of the whole world. You have now, as an eternal memorial of these, Your highest blessings, instituted and ordained this holy, most venerable Sacrament through Your almighty and blessed Word. In this Sacrament, You give us here in this Christian assembly Your true, essential body and blood, present with the blessed and unaltered bread and wine, to eat and to drink for the forgiveness of our sins. Through such true imparting and receiving of Your most holy body and blood, You unite us truly with Yourself, preparing our poor mortal and perishable bodies for the certain resurrection from the dead and for the glory of Your body and eternal life.

I pray to You, dearest and most precious treasure, Lord Jesus Christ, help me and grant me that I may receive this, Your most holy Sacrament, safely and beneficially for the salvation and blessing of my soul, so that I may thereby obtain all the blessings You have earned for my benefit; namely, the help and grace of Your most loving Father, the forgiveness of all my sins, righteousness, and eternal life, together with the Holy Spirit. Strengthen me in my weak faith toward You, increase my daily love toward my neighbor, and improve my entire life.

AMEN.

Psalm 111

Praise and thanks to the LORD with all my heart, In the council of the upright and in the assembly. Great are the works of the LORD; Whoever considers them has pure delight in them.

What He ordains is glorious and majestic, And His righteousness endures forever. He has established a memorial for His wonders, The gracious and merciful LORD.

He gives food to those who fear Him; He remembers His covenant forever. He makes known to His people His mighty deeds, That He may give them the inheritance of the nations.

The works of His hands are truth and justice; All His commandments are upright. They are upheld forever and ever; They are done in faithfulness and uprightness.

He sends redemption to His people; He promises that His covenant will remain forever. Holy and awesome is His name.

The fear of the LORD is the beginning of wisdom; This is sound understanding for all who follow it. His praise endures forever.

AMBROSIUS.

In hac disputatione, quod & quomodo panis cœnæ sit corpus Christi, non est quærendus naturæ ordo; cum idem illud corpus, non juxta naturæ ordinem, sed ex Spiritu Sancto conceptum, & ex virgine natum sit.

That is:

In this dispute, concerning that and how the bread of the Lord's Supper is Christ's body, we should not look to the course of nature, since that very body, against the course of nature, was conceived by the Holy Spirit and born of the Virgin.

AUGUSTINUS.

Demus, Deum aliquid posse, quod nos fateamur investigare non posse. In talibus rebus tota facti ratio, est potent a facientis.

That is:

Let us readily admit that God can do something which we must confess we cannot fathom. In this lies the entire foundation and reason of understanding, in that the One who does it is Almighty.

CHRYSOSTOMUS.

Hoc quod in poculo adest, meum est, quod ex latere Christi fluxit, & illud participamus.

That is:

That which is present in the chalice is precisely the same as that which flowed from the side of Christ, and this we receive.

DAMASCENUS.

Non est figura corporis & sanguinis Christi, sed est ipsum corpus Christi. Si quæris modum, nihil amplius scimus, quam quod verbum Domini est verum & efficax, & omnipotens: modus autem inscrutabilis.

That is:

It is not a figure or representation of the body and blood of Christ, but the body and blood of Christ itself. Do you ask how this happens? Concerning this, we cannot report more, other than that the Lord's Word is truthful, powerful, and almighty. The manner, however, how it happens, is unfathomable.

Made in the USA
Columbia, SC
23 December 2024